9204031

American STREAMLINE

DEPARTURES

American STREAMLINE

BERNARD HARTLEY & PETER VINEY

DEPARTURES

An intensive American English course for beginners
Student's Edition

American adaptation by Flamm/Northam Authors and Publishers Services, Inc.

Oxford University Press

Oxford University Press

200 Madison Avenue
New York, N.Y. 10016 USA

Walton Street
Oxford OX2 6DP England

OXFORD is a trademark of Oxford University Press.

© B. Hartley, P. Viney, and Oxford University Press 1983

First published 1983
Printing (last digit): 20

Library of Congress Cataloging in Publication Data

Hartley, Bernard.
  American streamline.

  "American adaptation by Flamn/Northam Authors
and Publishers Services, Inc."
  Includes index.
  Contents: (1) Departures.
  1. English language—Text-books for foreign
speakers. 2. English language—United States.
I. Viney, Peter. II. Title.
PE1128.H37 1983   428.2'4   82-24585
ISBN 0-19-434110-0(v. 1)
ISBN 0-19-434111-9(teacher's edition)
ISBN 0-19-434114-3(cassette)

Illustrations by:

Alun Burton	Dan Culhane
David English	Jack Fetchko for flex, Inc.
Dennis Kendrick	Paddy Mounter
Vantage Art, Inc.	Pete Kelly (cover)
David Ace	The Parkway Group
Jill Watkins	Michael Brownlow

Photographs by:
Beryl Goldberg

*The publishers would like to thank the following for their
time and assistance:*
Atlantic City Convention and Visitors Bureau,
Bloomsbury Restaurant Ltd., Briar Coffee Shop,
The Complete Traveller Bookshop, David's
Cookies, Flowertown Florist, Greco Shoe
Repair, Häagen-Dazs Ice Cream Shoppe,
Mad Jacs, Male Trend, Meta Photo Supply
Company, Pan Am, Raspberry International,
Redwood Empire Association Photo,
Terra Nova Cafe, Zenith Travel

Printed in Hong Kong

Students can buy a cassette which
contains a recording of the texts
and dialogs in this book.

1A Hello

Exercise 1

David Clark
Linda Rivera

He's David Clark.
She's Linda Rivera.

Alan Lee
Susan Lee

. . . .
. . . .

John Green
Carol Green

. . . .
. . . .

Exercise 2

Is she a teacher?
No, she isn't.
Is she a student?
Yes, she is.

. . . . a student?
No, ...
. . . . a teacher?
Yes, ...

1B Hello

Exercise 3

Is he from the
United States?
No, he isn't.
Where's he from?
He's from Canada.

. . . France?
No, ...
. . . ?
. . . Mexico.

. . . Brazil?
. . . .
. . . ?
. . . Japan.

Exercise 4

Are you a teacher?
. . . .
Are you a student?
. . . .
Are you from the
United States?
. . . .
Where are you
from?
. . . .

2A Excuse me!

I: Excuse me!
J: Yes?
I: Are you American?
J: Pardon me?
I: Are you from the United States?
J: Yes, we are.
I: Oh. I'm American too. Are you here on vacation?
J: No, we aren't. We're here on business.

J: Please sit down.
I: Thank you.

J: Coffee?
I: Yes, please.

J: Cream?
I: No, thanks.
J: Sugar?
I: Yes, please.

K: Where are you from?
I: I'm from Los Angeles.
K: Are you here on business?
I: No, I'm not. I'm on vacation.

2B Where are you from?

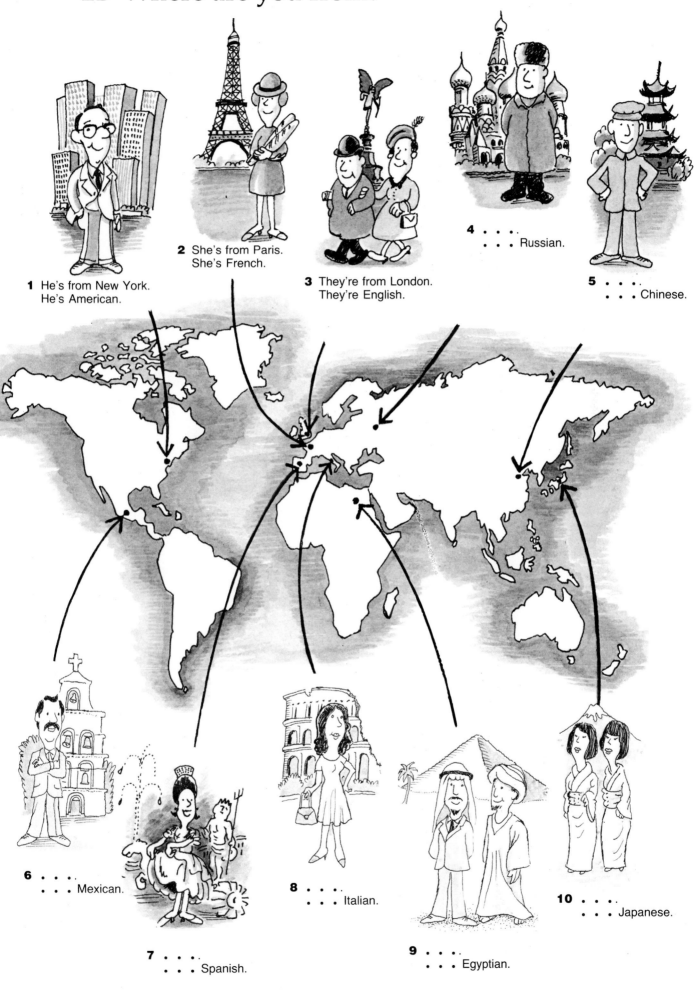

1 He's from New York.
He's American.

2 She's from Paris.
She's French.

3 They're from London.
They're English.

4 . . . .
. . . Russian.

5 . . . .
. . . Chinese.

6 . . . .
. . . Mexican.

7 . . . .
. . . Spanish.

8 . . . .
. . . Italian.

9 . . . .
. . . Egyptian.

10 . . . .
. . . Japanese.

3A What is it?

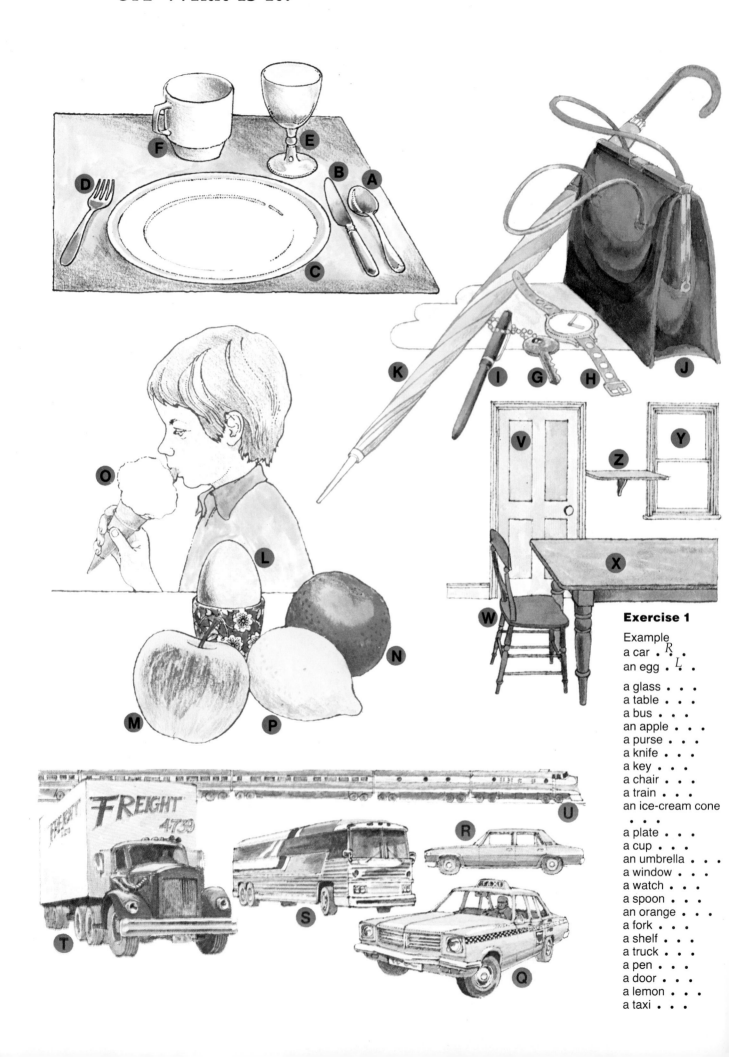

Exercise 1

Example
a car . R .
an egg . L .

a glass . . .
a table . . .
a bus . . .
an apple . . .
a purse . . .
a knife . . .
a key . . .
a chair . . .
a train . . .
an ice-cream cone
. . .
a plate . . .
a cup . . .
an umbrella . . .
a window . . .
a watch . . .
a spoon . . .
an orange . . .
a fork . . .
a shelf . . .
a truck . . .
a pen . . .
a door . . .
a lemon . . .
a taxi . . .

3B What are they?

Exercise 2

1 They're forks.
2 . . . .
3 . . . .
4 . . . .
5 . . . .
6 . . . .
7 . . . .
8 . . . .
9 . . . .
Use these words:
watches
cups
knives
keys
strawberries
cars
glasses
umbrellas

Exercise 3

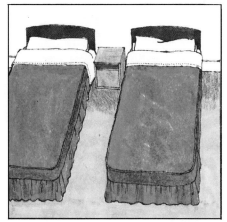

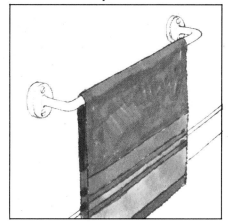

1 What is it?
It's a clock.

2 What are they?
They're radios.

3 . . . ?
. . . ashtray.

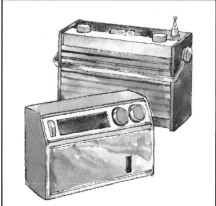

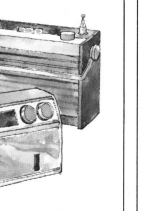

4 . . . ?
. . . beds.

5 . . . ?
. . . houses.

6 . . . ?
. . . towel.

4A What's your name?

Receptionist: Good evening, sir. May I help you?
Mr. Stern: Yes, thanks. This is my reservation.
Receptionist: What's your name?
Mr. Stern: Stern. My name's Thomas Stern.
Receptionist: Oh, yes, Mr. Stern. Room 15. Here's your key.
Mr. Stern: Thank you.

Bellman: Is this your suitcase?
Mr. Stern: No, it isn't.
Bellman: Oh, is that your suitcase over there?
Mr. Stern: Yes, it is.

Receptionist: Hello. May I help you?
Mr. Johnson: Yes, thank you.
Receptionist: What are your names, please?
Mr. Johnson: Mr. and Mrs. Paul Johnson.
Receptionist: Oh, yes. Here's your key.

Bellman: Are these your suitcases here?
Mrs. Johnson: No, they aren't.
Bellman: Oh, I'm sorry. Are those your suitcases over there?
Mrs. Johnson: Yes, they are.
Bellman: And are those your tennis rackets?
Mrs. Johnson: Yes, they are. Thank you.

Mrs. Johnson: Is this our room?
Mr. Johnson: What's the number?
Mrs. Johnson: 15.
Mr. Johnson: Oh, no, it isn't.
Mrs. Johnson: Is it number 13?
Mr. Johnson: No, it's not. That's our room—number 12.

4B What's your job?

Exercise 1

Look at 13.
What's his job?
He's a hotel
manager.

Look at 14.
What's her job?
She's a cashier.

Look at 15.
What are their
jobs?
They're waiters.

Look at 16.
. . . ?
. . . .

Look at 17.
. . . ?
. . . .

Look at 18.
. . . ?
. . . .

Look at 19.
. . . ?
. . . .

Use these words:

secretary
cooks
housekeeper
bellman

Exercise 2

Look at 20.
What's his job?
He's a pilot.

21 . . . ?
. . . .

22 . . . ?
. . . .

23 . . . ?
. . . .

24 . . . ?
. . . .

Use these words:

policemen
flight attendants
taxi driver
mechanic

Exercise 3

What's your name?
. . . .

What's your job?
. . . .

5A I'm cold

A: Brr!
B: Are you cold?
A: Yes, I am.
B: Well, I'm not. I'm hot!

C *It's big.* **D** *It's small.*

E . . . . **F** . . . .

G . . . . **H** . . . .

I . . . . **J** . . . .

K . . . **L** . . . .

M . . . **N** . . . .

O . . . . **P** . . . .

Q . . . . **R** . . . .

S . . . . **T** . . . .

U . . . . **V** . . . .

W . . . . **X** . . . .

Y . . . . **Z** . . . .

Use these words:
rich/poor	thick/thin	old/new
full/empty	cheap/expensive	tall/short
fat/thin	strong/weak	old/young
beautiful/ugly	long/short	

5B I'm cold

Exercise 1

1 Helen Wilson's *thirsty*.
2 Alan Wilson . . . .
3 Mrs. Wilson . . . .
4 Ms. Rossi . . . .
5 Mr. Parker . . . .
6 Mr. Lee . . . .
7 Mr. Adams
8 and Mr. Spencer . . . .

Use these words:
sad
angry
hungry
thirsty
tired
cold
hot

Big Joe Freezer   Steve King

Mrs. Loot   Fred Penny

Exercise 2

Now write four sentences for Big Joe Freezer (*He's fat*), Steve King, Mrs. Loot, Fred Penny.

Use these words:

rich	fat	old	big
poor	thin	young	small
tall	strong	beautiful	heavy
short	weak	ugly	light

6 There's a nice apartment

Janet: Hello.
Agent: Hello.
Janet: Is there an empty apartment in this building?
Agent: Yes, there is. There's a nice apartment on the fifth floor.
Janet: Are there two bedrooms?
Agent: No, there aren't. There's a living room, a small kitchen, and a very small bathroom.
Janet: And the bedroom?
Agent: Oh, there's a very large bedroom.
Janet: Is there a balcony?
Agent: No, there's no balcony.

Janet: Where's the kitchen?
Agent: Here it is.
Janet: Oh, it's very small.
Agent: Yes, but there's a stove, a refrigerator, and space for a dishwasher. There are some cabinets, and there's a shelf under the sink.
Janet: Are there any windows in the bathroom?
Agent: No, there aren't. But there are two large ones in the bedroom.
Janet: Good. It's a very nice apartment.

FLOOR PLAN

Exercise 1

sofa
There's a sofa *in the living room.*
radio
There's no radio *in the living room.*

Write sentences with:
1 telephone   **3** cabinet
2 chair   **4** table

Exercise 2

books
There are some books *on the shelf.*
cups
There aren't any cups *on the shelf.*

Write sentences with:
1 glasses   **3** magazines
2 records   **4** bottles

Exercise 3

telephone/table?
Is there a telephone *on the* table?
books/shelf
Are there any books *on the* shelf?

Write questions with:
1 radio/shelf
2 bottles/table
3 records/table

Exercise 4

Where are the bottles? They're on the shelf.
Where's the chair? It's in the living room.

Answer the questions:
1 Where's the television?
2 Where are the glasses?
3 Where are the books?
4 Where's the sofa?

7 Everyday conversation

A: Excuse me.
B: Yes?
A: Is there a post office near here?
B: Yes, there is.
A: Is it far?
B: No, it's not. Turn right at the first traffic light. It's on the left.
A: Thanks a lot.
B: You're welcome.

post office
bus stop
bank
coffee shop
telephone booth
supermarket
laundromat

first left
second right

C: Could you pass the salt, please?
D: Sure. Here it is.
C: Thanks.
D: And the pepper?
C: No, thanks.

salt
sugar
bread
catsup

pepper?
milk?
butter?
mustard?

E: Hi. A beer please.
F: Uh, are you eighteen?
E: Yes, I am.
F: O.K. Here you are.
E: Thanks. How much is that?
F: $1.15.

a beer
a Scotch
a bourbon
a double Scotch
  and soda
  and water
  and ice

$1.15
$2.15
$3.50

G: Could I have your phone number?
H: It's in the phone book.
G: What's your last name?
H: It's in the book too.
G: Very funny.
H: O.K. It's 679–7701.

679–7701
356–8022
296–2837
688–2119
836–6809
679–7300
549–6244

Mrs. Turner: Who's that? Who's that?

Tom: It's me . . . Tom.

Mrs. Turner: Tom?

Tom: Yes, Tom . . . your grandson, . . . from California!

Mrs. Turner: Oh, Tom! Come in!

Tom: This is my wife, Mary.

Mrs. Turner: Oh, how do you do?

Tom: . . . and these are our children, Jimmy and Nancy.

Mrs. Turner: Hello, Jimmy. Hello, Nancy. Well, this is a nice surprise!

Look at Mrs. Turner. Her skirt's black. Her blouse is white.
Look at Tom. His jacket's brown. His trousers are gray.
Look at Mary. Her dress is pink. Her shoes are orange.
Look at Jimmy. His shirt's red. His shorts are green.
Look at Nancy. Her T-shirt's yellow. Her jeans are blue.

Exercise 1

Captain Adams

Who's this?
It's Captain Adams.
He's an astronaut.

Mrs. Martin

Ms. Sanchez

Dr. Ross

Mr. Wong

Use these words: housewife/accountant/doctor/travel agent

Exercise 2

What color is it?
It's red.

9 Whose is it?

Mike: Hello, Barbara.
Barbara: Hello, Mike.
Mike: Wow! What's that?
Barbara: It's a Cadillac.
Mike: Hmmmm. Is it your car?
Barbara: Well, no . . . no, it isn't.
Mike: Whose car is it?
Barbara: It's Mr. Orson's car.
Mike: Mr. Orson? Who's he?
Barbara: He's my boss.
Mike: Is he a millionaire?
Barbara: Of course!

 1

 2

 3

 4

 5

6

 7

8

 9

 10

 11

Exercise 1

Who is it? It's Mr. Orson.
Write sentences for B and C.

Exercise 2

1 *What is it? It's a cigar.*
2 *What are they? They're glasses.*
Write sentences for 3–11.

Exercise 3

1 *Whose cigar is it?*
It's Mr. Orson's cigar.
2 *Whose glasses are they?*
They're Mike's glasses.
Write sentences for 3–11.

Look at this:

Look at Dick.
He's Anne's husband.
He's John's father.

Look at Anne.
She's Dick's wife.
She's Sue's mother.

Look at John.
He's their son.
He's Sue's brother.

Look at Sue.
She's their daughter.
She's John's sister.

10 Is there any sugar in the bowl?

There's some milk in the glass.
There's some sugar in the bowl.
There's some oil in the bottle.
There's some water in the pitcher.
There's some honey in the jar.
There's some rice in the box.

There are some apples on the table.
There are some eggs on the table.
There are some oranges on the table.
There are some bananas on the table.
There are some lemons on the table.
There are some onions on the table.

Exercise

 There isn't any butter.

 There isn't any cheese.

There isn't any beer.

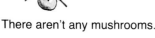 There aren't any tomatoes.

There aren't any mushrooms.

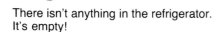 There aren't any eggs.

There isn't anything in the refrigerator.
It's empty!

Is there any cheese in the refrigerator?
Yes, there is.

Is there any butter in the refrigerator?
No, there isn't.

Are there any eggs in the refrigerator?
Yes, there are.

Are there any tomatoes in the refrigerator?
No, there aren't.

 butter

A There's some butter in the freezer.
B How much is there?
A There's a lot.

Write conversations with:
ice cream
meat

 hamburgers

A There are some hamburgers in the freezer.
B How many are there?
A There are a lot.

Write conversations with:
peas
pizzas

11 An American restaurant

Customer: Waiter! I'd like the menu, please.
Waiter: Here you are, sir.
Customer: Thanks . . . I'd like some soup . . . .
Waiter: Tomato soup?
Customer: Yes, . . . and I'd like a steak.
Waiter: Rare, medium, or well done?
Customer: Medium, please.
Waiter: Which vegetables would you like?
Customer: I'd like some potatoes, some peas, and a salad.
Waiter: Certainly, sir.
Customer: Oh, and I'd like some wine.
Waiter: Which wine would you like, sir?
Customer: A glass of red wine, please.

MENU

APPETIZERS
Onion Soup .... $1·90
Tomato Soup .... 1·50
Melon .... 2·00
Tomato Juice .... 1·00

ENTREES, MAIN COURSES
Sirloin Steak .... $9·00
Roast Beef .... 8·70
Fried Chicken .... 7·90
Broiled Lamb Chops ... 9·60
Filet of Sole .... 7·50
Ham Omelette .... 5·30
Cheese Omelette ...... 4·60

VEGETABLES
Baked Potato
French Fried Potatoes ... $1·00
Peas .... 1·00
Cauliflower .... ·80
Carrots .... ·90
Green Beans .... ·70
SALADS
Spinach .... ·60
Mixed Green

DESSERTS
Ice Cream .... $1·40
Apple Pie .... 1·60
Chocolate Cake .... 1·30
BEVERAGES
Coffee .... $·80
Tea .... ·60
Cola .... ·70

12 Do this! Don't do that!

Look at these pictures.

LOOK AT ME

LOOK AT HER

LOOK AT HIM

LOOK AT THEM

LOOK AT US

LOOK AT IT

Charles Orson is a film director. He's in the studio. He's with Steve Newman and Raquel Evans. Steve's an actor. Raquel's an actress. They're film stars.

"Everybody! Be quiet, please! O.K., Steve, now open the door . . . come in . . . walk to the sofa . . . . Walk! Don't run! . . . O.K., sit down . . . don't move . . . now, take Raquel's hand . . . look into her eyes . . . don't laugh! . . . smile!

Raquel! Smile at Steve . . . look into his eyes . . . don't laugh! . . . now, close your eyes. Steve! Kiss her! That's fine! Now, Steve, go to the door . . . go out, and close the door . . . O.K., turn the lights on . . . turn the microphones on . . . start the camera . . . action!"

Exercise

TURN THE RECORD PLAYER OFF!

13 Rob Dillon isn't happy

Look at this man. He's Rob Dillon. He's a rock star. He's very rich and famous.
Look at his house. It's large and expensive, and there's a swimming pool in the backyard. There are ten bedrooms in the house.
Rob's car is a 1983 Lincoln Continental. It's fast and comfortable. In his car there's a radio, a stereo cassette player, a bar, a cigarette lighter, and automatic windows.
But Rob isn't happy. He'd like a Rolls-Royce.

Look at this man. He's Chuck Stevenson. He's an English teacher. He's very poor, and he's not famous.
Look at his house. It's small and cheap, and there's no backyard. There are only two small bedrooms in the house.
Chuck's car is a 1969 Ford. It's slow and uncomfortable. There's no radio or cassette player in his car. There's an engine, a steering wheel, and there are four wheels and two doors.
Chuck isn't happy. He'd like a new Ford, a new job, and a new life.

Exercise

Rob's a rock star	Chuck's an English teacher.
Rob's famous.	• • •
Rob's house is large and expensive.	• • •
He'd like a Rolls-Royce.	• • •

14 My daddy can do everything!

Sally: My daddy's really wonderful. He's big and strong and handsome.

Annie: Really? Well, *my* daddy can do everything.

Sally: Can he? What?

Annie: He's really smart. He can speak a hundred languages.

Sally: A hundred! Which languages can he speak?

Annie: Well, he can speak Spanish, Italian, French, German, Japanese, Arabic, and, uh, a lot more.

Sally: Well, my daddy is athletic.

Annie: Athletic?

Sally: Uh huh. He can swim, ski, and play football, tennis, and baseball.

Annie: Oh, well, can your daddy cook?

Sally: What? No, he can't.

Annie: My daddy is a wonderful cook.

Sally: Really?

Annie: Yes, and he can sew and iron, too.

Sally: Oh. My daddy can't do that. But my mommy is beautiful and smart and she can . . .

Questions

1 Is Sally's father big?
2 Is he ugly?
3 Can he play football?
4 Can he sew?
5 Can he ski?
6 Can he cook?
7 Is Annie's father athletic?
8 Is he smart?
9 Can he speak Arabic?
10 Can he play tennis?
11 Can he iron?
12 Is Sally's mother smart?

Exercise

Example:
I can swim, but I can't ski.

Write ten sentences.

15 Everyday conversation

I: Please come in.
J: Thank you.
I: Sit down. Make yourself comfortable.
J: Thanks.
I: Would you like a cup of coffee?
J: Yes, please.
I: How about a cookie?
J: No, thanks. I'm on a diet.

a cup of coffee
a cup of tea
a glass of milk
a glass of wine
a glass of water

a cookie
a sandwich
a piece of cake
a piece of fruit
a piece of candy

K: Excuse me . . .
L: Yes, can I help you?
K: I'd like some information about the trains.
L: Where to?
K: Boston.
L: When?
K: Tomorrow.
L: Morning or afternoon?
K: Evening. About six o'clock.
L: O.K. There's one at 6:40.
K: Thanks.

trains
buses
planes
limousines

M: I'd like a pair of shoes, please.
N: What color would you like?
M: Brown.
N: What size are you?
M: Six. Can I try them on?
N: Yes, of course.

a pair of shoes
a pair of jeans
a pair of slacks
a pair of boots
a sweater
a jacket
a raincoat

O: How about dinner tonight?
P: Great! I'd love to.
O: Where can we meet?
P: How about Barney's Restaurant?
O: All right. What time?
P: Is seven o'clock O.K.?
O: Sure, that's fine.
P: Good. See you later.

dinner
a movie
a walk
a concert
a drink

16 Diana Rich, Tom Atkins, and Mike Jackson

Hi there, fans. My name's Diana Rich. I'm a famous actress — a superstar! I'm from New York. I have an apartment in New York and a house in Hollywood with a swimming pool and a tennis court. I have a new Mercedes and a lot of money in the bank. I have a husband and three wonderful·children in Hollywood. I have everything. Life's great!

Hello. My name's Tom Atkins. I'm from New York too. I'm broke. I don't have any money. I don't have a job or a car. I don't have a wife, and I don't have anything. Life's really terrible!

Look at this man. His name's Mike Jackson. He's not from New York. He's from Detroit. He's a factory worker. He has a good job. He has a car. He doesn't have a big house, but he has a nice apartment. He has a wife, but he doesn't have any children. Life's all right.

Exercise 1

Example: house in Hollywood
Does she have a house in Hollywood?
Yes, she does.

1 swimming pool
2 tennis court
3 Mercedes
4 husband

Exercise 3

Example:
brother   *I have a* brother.
Mercedes *I don't have a* Mercedes.

Write four sentences:
1 passport   3 motorcycle
2 watch   4 color TV

Exercise 2

Example: a job
Does he have a job? *No, he doesn't.*

1 a house
2 a car
3 a wife
4 any money
5 any children

Exercise 4

Answer these questions, with *Yes, I do* or *No, I don't.*

1 Do you have a car?
2 Do you have a passport?
3 Do you have any children?
4 Do you have a watch?
5 Do you have any money?

Questions

1 What's his name?
2 Where's he from?
3 Does he have a good job?
4 Does he have a car?
5 Does he have a big house?
6 Does he have a wife?
7 Does he have any children?

17 At customs

Customs Officer: Good morning. May I see your passport?

Ralph: Sure. Here it is.

C.O.: Thank you. Hmmm. O.K. Do you have anything to declare?

Ralph: Yes, I do.

C.O.: What do you have?

Ralph: I have some liquor and some cigarettes.

C.O.: How much liquor do you have?

Ralph: One bottle.

C.O.: O.K. And how many cigarettes do you have?

Ralph: A carton.

C.O.: Fine. What about perfume? Do you have any perfume?

Ralph: No, I don't.

C.O.: Good. Now open your suitcase, please.

Ralph: Huh? What?

C.O.: Open your suitcase. Now, let's see. Well, look at this. You have three bottles of liquor, four hundred cigarettes, and a lot of perfume.

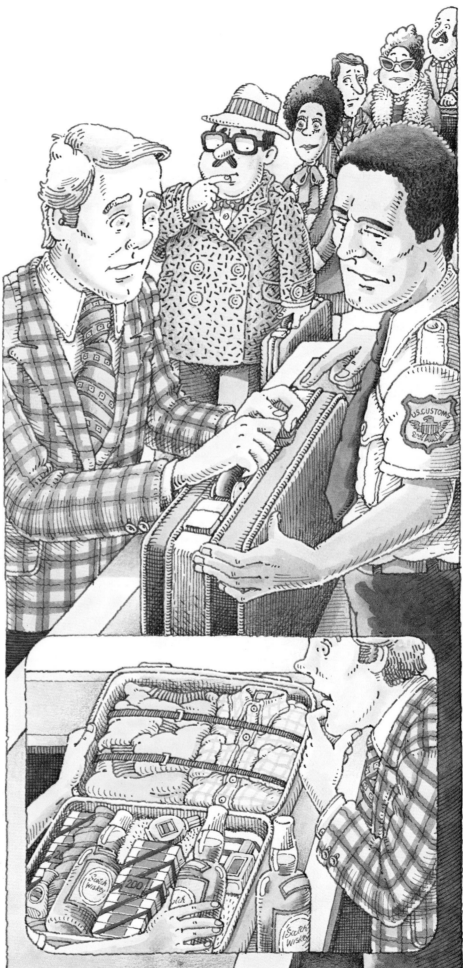

Questions

1 Does Ralph have anything to declare?
2 Does he have any cigarettes?
3 Ask, "How many?"
4 Does he have any perfume?
5 Ask, "How much?"
6 Does he have any bottles of liquor?
7 Ask, "How many?"

Exercise

How much wine *does she have?*
How many cameras *does she have?*
Write four questions:
1 . . . perfume . . . ?
2 . . . money . . . ?
3 . . . cigarettes . . . ?
4 . . . watches . . . ?

18 Which one?

George: How about some more wine?
Charles: Thanks.
George: Which glass is yours?
Charles: That one's mine.
George: Which one?
Charles: The empty one!

Charles: Good night and thanks for a lovely evening.
George: Now, which coats are yours?
Charles: Oh, those coats are ours.
George: Which ones?
Charles: The black one and the gray one.
George: Ah, yes . . .
Charles: Good. The gray one's mine, and the black one's hers.

Exercise 1

Which one would you like?
I'd like the classical one.

Exercise 2

Which ones would you like?
I'd like the expensive ones.

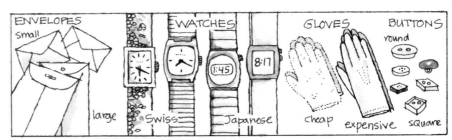

Exercise 3

Which house is theirs?
The big one's theirs.

Which house is his?
The small one's his.

Exercise 4

Example:
It's my pen.   *It's mine.*
They're our books.   *They're ours.*

1 It's his car . . . .
2 It's their house . . . .
3 It's John's coat . . . .
4 It's her hat . . . .
5 It's your house . . . .
6 It's Mary's bag . . . .

19 Everyday conversation

O: Can you show me some cameras, please?
P: Sure. What make do you want?
O: I'd like a Minolta.
P: This one's very good.
O: It looks good. How much is it?
P: $180.
O: Oh, that's too expensive.
P: How much can you spend?
O: About $100.
P: Here's one for $99.50.
O: Great! Can you show it to me?

cameras (Minolta)
radios (RCA)
watches (Timex)
cassette recorders (Sony)
color TVs (Zenith)

$180/$100/$99.50
$85/$72/$63
$52/$20/$18.75
$400/$300/$250

Q: Oh, excuse me! Waiter!
R: Yes?
Q: Could you bring us some more coffee, please?
R: Yes, right away.
Q: And could you bring us the check, please? We're in a hurry.

coffee
tea
cream
water
brandy

S: Good morning. Can I see your ticket, please?
T: Yes. Here it is.
S: O.K. And do you have any luggage?
T: Yes. One suitcase.
S: You can put it here.
T: Can I carry it with me on the plane? It isn't heavy.
S: No, I'm sorry. You can't. It's the wrong size.

Good morning
Good afternoon
Good evening
Hello

luggage
suitcases
bags

U: Good night, Andy.
V: Good night, Marilyn.
U: Have a wonderful vacation.
V: Thanks.
U: Don't forget . . . send me a postcard.
V: O.K. Wait a minute. I don't have your address.
U: That's O.K. You can send it to me at the office.
V: All right. Bye.
U: Bye.

vacation
trip
time

at the office
at school
at work
here

20 A postcard

Dear John,

This is a picture of Mexico City. The weather's beautiful. The hotel's excellent. There's a color TV and a refrigerator in my hotel room. The food is very good. Mexico City isn't expensive. My Spanish is terrible, but the people are friendly.

See you soon.

Best wishes,
Mary

HOTEL MARIA ISABEL
VISTA NOCTURNA
MEXICO, D. F.

EDITORIAL MEXICO, S. A.
GREETING CARDS CREATED BY FISCHGRUND

Mr. John Carter
167 Woodley Road
Cleveland, Ohio 44101
U.S.A.

Dear   Joe,
Anne,
Mom,
Dad,

| This is a picture of | Boston.
San Francisco.
Phoenix.
Miami. | The weather's | hot.
cold.
sunny.
rainy. | The school is very | good.
bad.
large.
small. | I'm in |

| a beginning
an intermediate
an advanced
a composition | class. There are a lot of | Koreans
Egyptians
Mexicans
Japanese | in my class. My | teacher's
best friend's
roommate's
advisor's | name is |

| Michael.
Pat.
David.
Sue. | English is very | easy.
difficult.
interesting. | The city's | boring.
exciting.
busy.
big. | There are a lot of | bars,
discos,
beaches,
parks, | and |

| things are very | cheap.
expensive. | The food is | different,
terrible,
delicious,
O.K., | and Americans are very | friendly.
reserved.
warm.
cold. | See you |

soon.
in 3 weeks.
in 4 weeks.
in 6 weeks.

Best wishes,
Love,
As ever,
Sincerely,

21 What are they doing?

Anne: Hello, Linda. Is Jack here?
Linda: No, he isn't.
Anne: Is he working today?
Linda: No, he isn't working today. He's in the kitchen.
Anne: What's he doing?
Linda: He's cooking.
Anne: What are you doing?
Linda: I'm reading.

Look at the picture.
They're in the nightclub now.

Exercise 1

He's smoking . *B* . .
He's drinking . . .
She's singing . . .
He's sleeping . . .
They're dancing . . .
They're eating . . .

Exercise 2

G *What's he doing? He's writing.*
H . . . .
I . . . .
J . . . .
drawing/typing/reading

Exercise 3

swimming/eating
He's swimming.
She isn't swimming.
Is she eating? *Yes, she is.*
Is he eating? *No, he isn't.*

reading/writing
. . . .
. . . .
. . . .

Look at these words:

work	working	smoke	smoking
cook	cooking	dance	dancing
read	reading	write	writing
eat	eating	type	typing
drink	drinking		
sing	singing	sit	sitting
sleep	sleeping	run	running
draw	drawing	swim	swimming

22 Can you help me?

Carlos is a student. He's staying with the Flynns, a family in Boston.

Carlos: Mrs. Flynn, can you help me? I'm doing my homework, and I can't understand this word.

Mrs. Flynn: Which one? Oh, that's difficult. I'm sorry, Carlos. I can't help you now. I'm watching TV. I can help you later.

Carlos: Oh? What are you watching?

Mrs. Flynn: I'm watching a good Western with John Wayne.

Carlos: Can Mr. Flynn help me?

Mrs. Flynn: Well, no, he can't. Not now. He's reading.

Carlos: What's he reading?

Mrs. Flynn: He's reading a magazine.

Carlos: What about Kate?

Mrs. Flynn: Oh, she can't help you now. She's talking on the phone.

Carlos: Who's she talking to?

Mrs. Flynn: I don't know. You're asking a lot of questions tonight, Carlos!

Carlos: Yes, I know. I'm practicing my English.

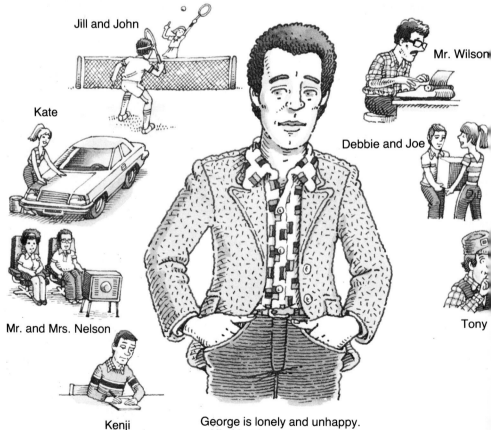

Jill and John

Kate

Mr. Wilson

Debbie and Joe

Mr. and Mrs. Nelson

Kenji

Tony

George is lonely and unhappy.
His friends are busy today.

Exercise

Jill and John/tennis.
What are Jill and John *doing?*
They're playing tennis.

Mr. and Mrs. Nelson/television
Kate/her car
Mr. Wilson/a letter
Kenji/a letter
Debbie and Joe/a box
Tony/coffee

watching
drinking
carrying
washing
writing
typing

23 Everyday conversation

A: Would you like to come to a party?

B: Well, uh, I'd like to. When is it?

A: Saturday night.

B: Sorry. I'm busy on Saturday.

A: What are you doing?

B: I'm doing my homework.

A: Your homework? Really? Well, maybe some other time.

B: Yeah, thanks anyway.

party
dance
picnic
rock concert
football game

Saturday
Sunday
Monday
Tuesday
Wednesday
Thursday
Friday

C: Excuse me. Is this seat taken?

D: No, it isn't.

C: Is it O.K. if I sit here?

D: Yes, of course.

C: Uh, is that your newspaper?

D: Yes, it is.

C: May I borrow it for a minute?

D: Yes, sure.

newspaper
pen
lighter
magazine

E: Good morning.

F: Good morning. Can I help you?

E: Well, I'm looking for a textbook.

F: What's the title?

E: *Instant English.* Do you have it?

F: Yes. It's on this shelf.

E: How much is it?

F: $6.00.

E: May I see it, please?

F: Of course. Here you are.

E: Thank you.

F: Your English is very good. Are you studying it?

E: No. I'm teaching it.

book
  (*Instant English*)
record
  (*Grease*)
magazine
  (*Time*)
cassette
  (*Instant English*)
dictionary
  (*Oxford Picture Dictionary*)

$6.00
$6.25
$1.50
$12.95
$14.00

G: Can I help you?

H: Pardon me?

G: Can I help you?

H: Oh, no thanks, I'm just looking.

24 The fashion show

And now, ladies and gentlemen, here's Julia. Julia's wearing a white cotton blouse and a black wool skirt. She's wearing orange shoes, and she's carrying an orange leather bag with a gold chain. Isn't she lovely? Thank you, Julia.

Now here's Wayne. He's wearing dark blue denim pants and a light blue polyester sport coat. He's wearing a yellow cotton shirt and a red wool tie. Thank you, Wayne.

TONY   JUNE

SUNGLASSES

A SILVER CHAIN

PURPLE T-SHIRT

BLACK SHORTS

WHITE SOCKS

RUNNING SHOES

GOLD EARRINGS

NECKLACE

LIGHT PINK BLOUSE

TAN LEATHER BELT

DIAMOND RING

DARK PINK SKIRT

TAN BOOTS

Exercise

Write sentences about Tony and June.

25 Going to the movies

Pete's standing outside the movie theater. He's waiting for his friend Betsy. He's looking at his watch because she's late. An old man's coming out of the theater. A young woman's going into the theater. A boy's running up the steps. A woman's buying a ticket from the cashier. Some people are standing in line outside the movie theater.

Questions

Where's Pete standing?
Who's he waiting for?
What's he looking at?
Why is he looking at his watch?
Who's coming out of the theater?
Who's going into the theater?
Where's the boy running?
Where are the people standing in line?

Now Pete's in the theater with Betsy. He's sitting between Betsy and a man with a mustache. A woman's sitting in front of him. She's wearing a hat, and Pete can't see the movie. A man's sitting behind Pete. He's smoking a cigarette. Betsy's angry because the smoke's getting in her eyes. And it's illegal!

Questions

Where's Pete now?
Who's he with?
Where's he sitting?
Who's sitting in front of him?
Why can't Pete see the movie?
Who's sitting behind him?
What's the man smoking?
Why is Betsy angry?

This is a scene from the movie. In this scene, a beautiful young woman's lying across the tracks. She's shouting "Help!" because a train's coming along the tracks. It's very near. It's coming round the bend now. HELP!

Questions

Where's the woman lying?
What's she shouting?
Why is she shouting?
Is the train near?
Can you see the train?
Where is it?

26 What's on television tonight?

Anne: Hi, John. I'm home.
John: Hi. How are you?
Anne: I'm tired. How about you?
John: I'm tired too.
Anne: What time is it?
John: It's a quarter to six.
Anne: What's on television tonight?
John: There's a good program on at a quarter after eight. "Kris Kristofferson in Concert."
Anne: Yes, . . . and there's a good movie on after the six o'clock news.
John: Oh, wait a minute. There's a football game on at seven.
Anne: Oh, I can't watch that. There's a comedy special on at seven on Channel 7.
John: But, Anne, it's my favorite team. It's a very important game.
Anne: Well, I can watch my programs on the portable TV in the bedroom.

TV Page

Tuesday
6 PM to 10 PM

6:00 (2) NEWS: Dan Rather
(7) I LOVE LUCY
(5) NEWS: Harry Reasoner
(13) SESAME STREET

6:30 (2) P.M. MAGAZINE
(7) THREE'S COMPANY
(13) YOU CAN GROW HOUSEPLANTS

6:45 (5) MOVIE: Roman Holiday
(13) MacNEIL/LEHRER REPORT

7:00 (2) PROFESSIONAL FOOTBALL:
From Washington, D.C. The Washington Redskins vs. The Miami Dolphins

(7) SPECIAL: BOB HOPE
Guests: Raquel Welch, Joe Namath

7:30 (13) CLOSE UP: Japan Today

8:15 (7) KRIS KRISTOFFERSON
(13) ROYAL CANADIAN BALLET: Swan Lake

8:45 (7) HILL STREET BLUES
(5) THAT'S INCREDIBLE

9:00 (2) HART TO HART

9:15 (5) QUINCY

10:00 (5) LOCAL NEWS
(7) TV MOVIE: The Shadow Rider

(13) DICK CAVETT: Interview with Truman Capote

International time

It's one o'clock in Mexico City

New York

Caracas

Rio de Janeiro

Greenland

The Azores

London

Rome

Istanbul

Baghdad

Abu Dhabi

Karachi

Exercise

What time is it? . . . .
It's three o'clock.

27 In prison

Tim: Well, tomorrow we're going to leave this place!

Fred: Yes. What are you going to do first?

Tim: Well, I'm going to rent a big car, meet my girlfriend, and take her to an expensive restaurant. We're going to have lobster and champagne. What about you, Fred?

Fred: My wife's going to meet me outside the prison. Then we're going to visit her mother.

Tim: Your mother-in-law? You're kidding!

Fred: No, I'm not. I'm going to work for my wife's mother.

Tim: Really? You're not going to work for your mother-in-law!

Fred: Well, she has a little hamburger place in Chicago.

Tim: What are you going to do there?

Fred: I'm going to be a dishwasher.

Tim: What? Wash dishes? Well, I'm not going to work. I'm going to have a good time!

Fred: You're lucky. I'm going to rob a bank next week.

Tim: Are you crazy? Why?

Fred: Because I'm happy in prison!

Exercise 1

prison

He's going to leave prison.

Write sentences with:
1 car
2 girlfriend
3 good time

Tim

Exercise 2

car

He isn't going to rent a car.

Write sentences with:
1 lobster
2 champagne
3 good time

Fred

Exercise 3

lobster

They're going to have lobster.

Write sentences with:
1 car
2 champagne
3 good time

Tim and his girlfriend

Exercise 4

champagne

They aren't going to have champagne.

Write sentences with:
1 good time
2 lobster
3 car

Fred and his wife

28 A wedding

1
This is a traditional church wedding. The bride and groom are leaving the church. She's wearing a long white gown and carrying a bunch of flowers. The groom is wearing a tuxedo and a red carnation. He's holding her hand. Their friends and relatives are throwing rice. The bride and groom are both smiling because they're very happy.

1 What is this?
2 What are the bride and groom doing?
3 What's the bride wearing?
4 What's she carrying?
5 What's the groom wearing?
6 What's he holding?
7 What are their friends doing?
8 Why are the bride and groom smiling?

2
In a few minutes, they're all going to drive to a hotel for the reception. They're going to have cocktails and dinner. Then they're going to drink champagne, and the bride and groom are going to cut the cake. Some people are going to make speeches. Then everyone is going to dance.

1 Where are they all going to drive to?
2 What are they going to have?
3 Then what are they going to drink?
4 What are the bride and groom going to do?
5 What are some people going to do?
6 What's everyone going to do then?

3
Later on, the bride and groom are going to leave the reception and drive to Kennedy Airport. They're going to fly to Mexico for their honeymoon.
Tonight, the bride's parents are going to say, "We're not losing a daughter. We're getting a son."

1 When are the bride and groom going to leave the reception?
2 Where are they going to drive?
3 Where are they going to fly?
4 What are the bride's parents going to say?

29 Computer dating

Interviewer: Hello. Come in, please.

Mr. Mattox: Uh, good afternoon. My name's Mattox . . . George Mattox. I'm — uh — looking for a woman friend.

Interviewer: Please sit down, Mr. Mattox. First, I have some questions for you.

Mr. Mattox: What about?

Interviewer: Well, about music, for example. Do you like music?

Mr. Mattox: Yes, I do. I like classical music and jazz.

Interviewer: Do you like foreign food?

Mr. Mattox: No, I don't. I like meat and potatoes.

Interviewer: How old are you, Mr. Mattox?

Mr. Mattox: What? Listen, young man. I don't like these personal questions!

Interviewer: Oh, well, uh, can you fill out this form later and mail it to me?

Mr. Mattox: No. I can find my own friends.

Interviewer: Wait, Mr. Mattox. There are two very interesting women . . .

Mr. Mattox: Well, O.K. I'm 65 years old. I like TV, but I don't like movies. I like animals, but I don't like children.

Exercise 1

Look at George Mattox:
Does he like jazz?
Write 5 questions.

Exercise 2

Do you like football?
Write 5 questions.

Exercise 3

Look at Mary Ellen Turner.
1 She likes animals.
2 She doesn't like movies.
Write 10 sentences about her.

Exercise 4

1 I like movies.
2 I don't like dogs.
Write 10 sentences about yourself.

Computer Dating Service, Inc.

Please print

Name _George Mattox_
Address _45 Dent St. N.Y._
Telephone _(212) 531-9467_
Birthdate _December 11, 1918_
Occupation _Teacher_
Marital status _Single_

LIKES _TV, Animals_
Colors _blue, brown, purple_
Food _Meat and potatoes_
Hobbies _fishing, golf_

Music _Classical and jazz_

DISLIKES _movies, children, foreign food_

George Mattox
Signature

Computer Dating Service, Inc.

Please print

Name _Mary Ellen Turner_
Address _4 Union St. N.Y._
Telephone _(212) 966-1692_
Birthdate _May 15, 1921_
Occupation _homemaker_
Marital status _widow_

LIKES _animals_
Colors _red, white, blue_
Food _steak_
Hobbies _knitting, reading, watching TV_
Music _classical_

DISLIKES _football, rock, movies_

Mary Ellen Turner
Signature

30 I love you, Jacqueline

Larry: Please marry me, Jacqueline. I want you. I need you. I love you.

Jackie: I'm sorry, Lawrence, but I can't.

Larry: Oh, Jackie, why not?

Jackie: Well, Larry. I like you . . . I like you a lot . . . but, I don't love you.

Larry: But Jackie, love isn't everything.

Jackie: Oh, Larry, you don't understand . . . for me love is everything.

Larry: Do you . . . love another man, Jackie?

Jackie: Yes, Larry, I do.

Larry: Not Michael Kennedy?

Jackie: Yes, Michael Kennedy.

Larry: But he doesn't want you. He's engaged.

Jackie: I know.

Larry: But Jackie, Mike isn't a rich man. I can give you everything. What do you want? Clothes? Money? Travel? A house in Palm Beach?

Jackie: No, Larry. I don't want those things. I only want Mike.

Questions

Who wants Jackie?
Does he love her?
Does Jackie like Larry?
Does she like him a lot?
Does she love him?
Does Jackie love another man?
What's his name?
Does Mike want Jackie?
Is he rich?
Is Larry rich?
What can he give Jackie?
Does she want clothes?
Does she want money?
What does she want?

Exercise 1

Who wants Jackie?
Larry wants Jackie.

Who loves Jackie?
Who needs Jackie?
Who wants Mike?
Who loves Mike?

Exercise 2

Who does Larry want?
Larry wants Jackie.

Who does Larry love?
Who does Jackie love?
Who does Jackie want?
Who does Larry need?

31 Everyday conversation

G: What are you doing this weekend?
H: I'm going out of town.
G: Oh, where are you going?
H: I'm going to Las Vegas.
G: For how long?
H: Just for two days.

this weekend
on Saturday
on Sunday
tomorrow
next week

Las Vegas
Philadelphia
New Orleans
Acapulco
Fort Lauderdale
Quebec

I: Do you have a car?
J: Yes, I do.
I: What kind is it?
J: It's a Honda.
I: Do you like it?
J: Yes, I like it a lot.
I: Why?
J: Because it's very economical.

Honda
Ford
VW
Corvette
Dodge

economical
comfortable
efficient
convenient
fast

K: Excuse me.
L: Yes?
K: Do you have any change?
L: What do you need?
K: I need some quarters.
L: Sure. How many do you want?
K: Well, can you change a dollar bill?
L: Yes, I think so. Here are four quarters.

coins:
quarters (25¢)
dimes (10¢)
nickels (5¢)
pennies (1¢)

bills:
a dollar bill ($1)
a five-dollar bill ($5)
a ten-dollar bill ($10)
a twenty-dollar bill ($20)
a fifty-dollar bill ($50)
a hundred-dollar bill ($100)

M: Hello.
N: Hello. Can I help you?
M: Could you repair these boots?
N: Yes, sure. What's the problem?
M: They need new heels.
N: O.K. When do you need them?
M: As soon as possible.
N: Is Thursday afternoon O.K.?
M: Yes, that's fine.

these boots
        glasses
        shoes
this camera
        watch
        radio

Thursday afternoon
Saturday morning
Wednesday late afternoon

32 An interview

Arnold Rivera, the TV news reporter, is interviewing Mrs. Cornelia Vandergilt for the program *Real People*.

AR: Well, Mrs. Vandergilt, please tell our viewers about an ordinary day in your life.

CV: Well, I wake up at eight o'clock.

AR: Really? Do you get up then?

CV: No, of course I don't get up at that time. I have breakfast in bed, and I read the "New York Times."

AR: What time do you get up?

CV: I get up at ten.

AR: What do you do then?

CV: I read my letters and dictate the answers to my secretary.

AR: And then?

CV: At eleven I take a walk with Jimmy.

AR: Jimmy? Who's Jimmy?

CV: Jimmy's my dog.

AR: Oh. What time do you have lunch?

CV: I have lunch at twelve-thirty. I eat alone.

AR: Oh, I see. Well, what do you do after lunch?

CV: Oh, I rest until six o'clock.

AR: And at six? What do you do at six?

CV: I get dressed for dinner. I have dinner at seven o'clock.

AR: Yes, well, what do you do after dinner?

CV: I read or watch TV. I take a bath at nine-thirty, and I go to bed at ten.

AR: Thank you, Mrs. Vandergilt. You certainly have a busy and interesting life.

CV: You're welcome.

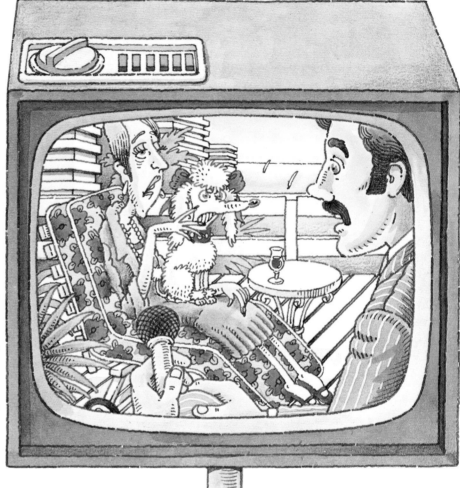

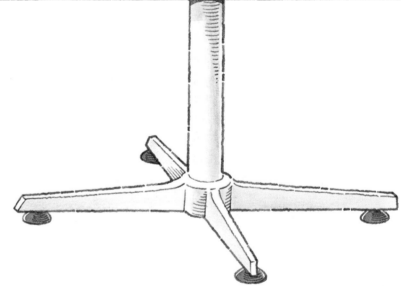

Questions

Who's interviewing Mrs. Cornelia Vandergilt?
Does she wake up at nine o'clock?
Ask, "What time?"
Does she have breakfast in the kitchen?
Ask, "Where?"
Does she read the "Los Angeles Times"?
Ask, "What?"
Does she read her letters?
Does she dictate the answers to her husband?

Does she walk in the garden with her secretary?
Ask, "Who with?"
Does she have lunch at twelve?
Ask, "What time?"
What does she do until six?
What does she do at six?
Does she have dinner at eight?
Ask, "What time?"
Does she go to bed at nine-thirty?
Ask, "What time?"

Exercise

A *She reads* the "New York Times."
B *She doesn't read* the "Los Angeles Times."
C *Does she read* "Time Magazine"?

A She walks with her dog.
B . . . with her secretary.
C . . . with her husband?

A She eats lunch alone.
B . . . with Jimmy.
C . . . with her husband?

33 Every day

1 Mac's a truck driver.
2 He's twenty-five years old.
3 He works five days a week.
4 He gets up at six o'clock every day.
5 He eats an enormous breakfast.
6 He drinks two cups of coffee.
7 Then he kisses his wife goodbye.
8 He leaves for work at six-thirty.
9 He has lunch at a hamburger place.
10 He comes home at five o'clock.
11 He has dinner and watches TV.
12 He goes to bed at ten o'clock.

Questions

1 What does Mac do?
2 How old is he?
3 How many days a week does he work?
4 What time does he get up?
5 What does he eat for breakfast?
6 What does he drink?
7 What does he do after breakfast?
8 What time does he leave for work?
9 Where does he have lunch?
10 What time does he come home?
11 What does he do in the evening?
12 What time does he go to bed?

Exercise

Now ask (and answer) questions about these people:

	JUDITH	PETER & PAUL	GREGORY
1	architect	students	oil company heir
2	35	12	42
3	the office/5 days a week	school/5 days a week	not/work/5 days a week
4	7:30	7:00	11:00
5	nothing	cereal	caviar
6	orange juice	milk	champagne
7	daughter	mother	fifth wife
8	the office/9:15	school/8:30	his club/12:00
9	in a coffee shop	in the cafeteria	at the Brown Hat Restaurant
10	home/6:00	home/4:00	not/come home
11	go out with friends	watch TV	go to the casino
12	midnight	nine o'clock	five o'clock in the morning

34 What's My Job?

Master of Ceremonies (MC): Good evening, ladies and gentlemen. Welcome to *What's My Job?* We have three famous people here — C. James Moore, the scientist; Bonita Moreno, the movie star; and Ken Carson, the rock star. They're going to ask the questions. Now here's our first contestant. First, Dr. Moore.

Dr. Moore: Umm, do you work outside?

Contestant: No, I don't.

Dr. Moore: I see. Do you work in an office?

Contestant: Well, yes. Yes, I do.

Dr. Moore: Do you wear a uniform?

Contestant: No, I don't.

MC: Next, Bonita Moreno.

Ms. Moreno: Oh, is your job important?

Contestant: Yes, it is.

Ms. Moreno: Do you get a big salary?

Contestant: Yes, I do.

Ms. Moreno: Do you have any special diplomas?

Contestant: Yes, I do.

MC: Thank you, Bonita. Now, Ken Carson.

Mr. Carson: Hello. Do you work with your hands?

Contestant: Yes, I do.

Mr. Carson: Do you work on weekends?

Contestant: No, I don't.

Mr. Carson: Do you travel?

Contestant: No, I don't.

MC: That's the ninth question! Now you can ask one last question.

Ms. Moreno: Are you a doctor?

Contestant: No, I'm not. I'm a dentist.

35 Never on Sunday

Reverend: Oh, hello there, Mr. Benson. I never see you in church nowadays.

Benson: Oh, well, uh, Reverend Wilson, that's true. But my wife always goes to church. She goes every Sunday.

Reverend: I know. But you never come.

Benson: Well, I rarely come . . . but I'm always there on Christmas and Easter.

Reverend: But what about Sundays, Mr. Benson?

Benson: Uh, I'm usually busy on Sundays. For example, I often wash my car on Sunday mornings.

Reverend: I see. Why don't you wash your car on Saturday next week?

Benson: Oh, I can't do that, Reverend.

Reverend: Why not?

Benson: It's my son's wedding day next Saturday. I'm going to church!

Exercise 1

He/sometimes/football.
He sometimes *plays* football.

1 They/often/potatoes.
2 She/usually/a skirt.
3 I/never/a hat.
4 He/occasionally/TV.
5 We/rarely/vodka.
6 You/never/cigars.

Exercise 2

coffee
I sometimes drink coffee.
or
I never drink coffee.
or
I often drink coffee.

Now write one true sentence for each:
1 coffee
2 TV
3 golf
4 spaghetti
5 wine
6 caviar
7 a newspaper
8 the movies
9 new clothes
10 a tie
11 cigarettes
12 rock music

1 Every morning he brushes his teeth. He *always* brushes his teeth in the morning.

2 She gets up at 7 o'clock from Monday to Saturday, but on Sunday she gets up at 11 o'clock. She *usually* gets up at 7 o'clock.

3 They like movies. They see all the new movies. They *often* go to the movies.

4 He's got a radio and a television. He *sometimes* listens to the radio, and he *sometimes* watches television.

5 Her brother lives in Texas. She doesn't. She sees him four or five times every year. She *occasionally* sees him.

6 He doesn't usually smoke, but at Christmas, after dinner, he has a cigar. He *rarely* smokes cigars.

7 She doesn't like coffee. She *never* drinks coffee.

36 A questionnaire

Arthur McNair works for a market research company in San Francisco. He's asking people about their free time:

AM: Excuse me, ma'am.

Janet Ross: Yes?

AM: I'm from Market Research, Inc. May I ask you some questions?

JR: Uh, yes, all right.

AM: Thank you. First, what time do you usually get home from work?

JR: Um, I usually get home about six o'clock.

AM: When do you usually have dinner?

JR: I usually eat about seven o'clock, but I sometimes eat at eight o'clock or nine o'clock. My husband works too!

AM: What do you usually do after dinner?

JR: Well, I sometimes go out, but I usually stay home and read or watch TV.

AM: How often do you go out?

JR: Oh, not often . . . about once or twice a week.

AM: Do you often see your friends?

JR: Yes, I do. Quite often. I sometimes visit them, and they sometimes visit me.

AM: Do you ever go to the movies?

JR: Oh, yes.

AM: How often?

JR: Well, I occasionally see a movie. I like horror movies . . . *Frankenstein* and *Dracula*.

AM: What about the theater? Do you ever go to the theater?

JR: Yes, I do, but not often. I rarely go to the theater.

AM: Do you ever go to the ballet?

JR: No, never. I don't like ballet.

AM: Well, thank you, Ms. Ross.

JR: May I ask you a question?

AM: Yes?

JR: What do you do in your spare time?

AM: I ask the questions, Ms. Ross. I don't answer them.

JR: Oh, I see.

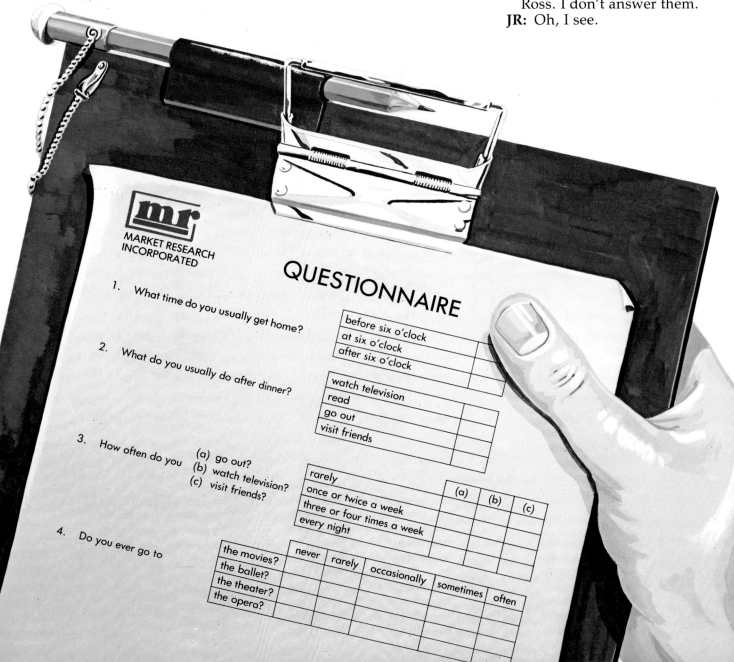

mr
MARKET RESEARCH INCORPORATED

QUESTIONNAIRE

1. What time do you usually get home?

before six o'clock	
at six o'clock	
after six o'clock	

2. What do you usually do after dinner?

watch television	
read	
go out	
visit friends	

3. How often do you (a) go out? (b) watch television? (c) visit friends?

	(a)	(b)	(c)
rarely			
once or twice a week			
three or four times a week			
every night			

4. Do you ever go to

	never	rarely	occasionally	sometimes	often
the movies?					
the ballet?					
the theater?					
the opera?					

37 What do they do every day?

Hello. My name's Douglas Hunter. I'm a pilot for Pan Am. I fly 747s. I'm not working today; I'm playing golf. It's my favorite sport.

Questions

What's his name?
What does he do?
What does he fly?
What's he doing now?
What's his favorite sport?

This man's a professional jockey. His name's Ricky Lopez. He rides racehorses. He isn't riding a racehorse at the moment. He's dancing with his sixth wife.

Questions

What's his name?
What does he do?
Who's he with right now?
What are they doing?

This is a picture of Joan and Dave. They teach English at a language school in San Francisco. They aren't teaching at the moment. They're in a restaurant. They're talking about their students.

Questions

Who are they?
What do they do?
Are they teaching right now?
Where are they?
What are they doing?

This is Cynthia Graham. She dances for the New York City Ballet. She isn't dancing now. She's taking a bath in her hotel room. Later she's going to dance at the White House for the President and his guests.

Questions

What's her name?
What does she do?
Is she dancing now?
What's she doing?
What's she going to do later?

Exercise

Reggie Johnson, baseball player

Example:
a *What does he do? He plays baseball.*

b *What's he doing now? He's sleeping.*

Kathleen and Kate, singers

a . . . .

b . . . .
. . . .

Lucy Dooley, artist

a . . . .

b . . . .
. . . .

38 Well or badly?

There's a baseball game on TV today. The New York Yankees are playing the Chicago White Sox. They are both good teams. They usually play well. But today the Yankees are playing very well, and the White Sox are playing badly.

Questions

What's on TV?
Which teams are playing?
Are they good teams?
Do they usually play well or badly?
How are the Yankees playing today?
How are the White Sox playing?

Tom Morgan often has accidents. This is his fourth accident this year. He's a bad driver because he's a fast and careless driver. He drives fast, carelessly, and badly.

Questions

What's his name?
Does he often have accidents?
Is this his first accident this year?
Is he a good or bad driver?
Does he drive well or badly?
Is he a fast or slow driver?
Does he drive carefully or carelessly?

John Gonzalez is an excellent driver. He always drives slowly, carefully, and well. All his friends say, "John's a good driver! He's very careful."

Questions

What's his name?
Is he a good driver or a bad driver?
Does he drive well or badly?
Is he a fast driver or a slow driver?
Does he drive carefully or carelessly?

Susan Yamakawa works very hard. She's a fast worker. Her boss often says, "Ms. Yamakawa works hard 8 hours a day. She's a hard worker and a good employee."

Questions

What's her name?
Is she a hard worker or a lazy worker?
Does she work hard or lazily?
Is she a fast or a slow worker?
Does she work fast or slowly?

Exercise

Kevin's a good player.
How does he play?
He plays well.

1 You're a bad swimmer.
2 She's a careful driver.
3 John's a slow learner.
4 They're hard workers.
5 He's a fast walker.

Look at this:

bad/badly	happy/happily	good/well
slow/slowly	busy/busily	fast/fast
careful/carefully	noisy/noisily	hard/hard
careless/carelessly		

39 Everyday conversation

O: How do you come to work?
P: By bus.
O: How long does it take?
P: Oh, about twenty minutes.
O: Do you usually get a seat?
P: Sometimes, but not often.

bus
train
subway

twenty minutes
an hour
half an hour
an hour and a half

Q: Is Maria Italian?
R: Yes, I think so.
Q: Does she speak English well?
R: No, I don't think so.
Q: Is she coming to the dance
tonight?
R: I hope so!

Italian
Portuguese
Venezuelan
Mexican
Egyptian

dance
party
disco
basketball game
get-together

S: What's the matter?
T: I have a bad cold.
S: Why don't you go to a
doctor?
T: I don't know any doctors.
S: Why don't you call Dr.
Perez? He's really great.
T: Thanks. That's a good idea.

a bad cold
a sore throat
a stomachache
a fever
a backache

great
fantastic
excellent
wonderful
competent

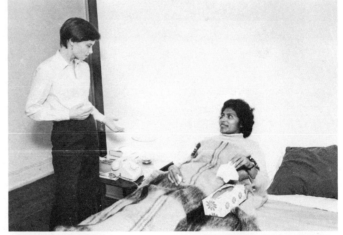

U: Would you like to dance?
V: Yes.
U: Do you come here often?
V: Sometimes.
U: Do you live near here?
V: No, I don't.
U: Where do you work?
V: In a bank.
U: Do you like it?
V: It's O.K.

sometimes
once a week
twice a week
every night
occasionally

a bank
a factory
a boutique
a beauty salon
a hospital

40 A personal letter

Pensión San Jose
Hamburgo 243
Zona Rosa
Mexico 5, D.F.
August 9

Dear John,
Well, this is my second week in Mexico City. I like it very much. I usually get up at 7 o'clock and have breakfast at my rooming house. Mexican breakfasts are very big, and the coffee's delicious. I always go to school by subway. I usually arrive at school at about 9 o'clock. I'm learning a lot of Spanish. School usually finishes at noon. In the evening I occasionally stay home and study, but I usually go out for dinner with a friend. Life is very interesting here. Next weekend I'm going to the Yucatán Peninsula. Give my regards to everybody.
Love, Mary xxx

Dear   Joe,
     Anne,
     Mom,
     Dad,

Well, this is my	second *third* *fourth*	week	on vacation. *in the United States.* *here.*	I	like it *don't like it*	very much. I	usually *always*

get up at	seven o'clock *7:30* *eight o'clock*	and have breakfast	with a friend. *in the hotel.* *in a coffee shop.*	American breakfasts are very	big. *small.* *good.*

I	sometimes *usually* *always*	go to school	by bus. *by subway.* *by car.*	I usually arrive at school at	nine *eleven* *one*	o'clock. In the

evenings I	usually *sometimes* *occasionally*	stay home, but	sometimes *usually* *occasionally*	I go out to	a concert *a disco* *a restaurant*	and

listen to music. *dance.* *talk to my friends.*	Life is very	busy *boring* *exciting*	here.	Tomorrow *Next week* *Next Sunday*	I'm going	to Detroit. *on a trip.* *to a rock concert.*

Give my	best wishes *regards* *love*	to	your parents. *Grandpa.* *the family.*

Love, *Fondly,* *Yours truly,* *Love and kisses,*

41 Where were you yesterday?

Detective: All right, Mr. Briggs. Where were you yesterday?
Briggs: Yesterday? What time?
Detective: At two o'clock. Where were you at two o'clock?
Briggs: Oh, I was at home.
Detective: You weren't at home. You were right here in New York City.
Briggs: No, I wasn't! I was at home in New Jersey. Ask my girlfriend. She was with me.
Detective: Well, we're going to speak to her later. Where is she now?
Briggs: Oh . . . I don't know.
Detective: O.K., now, where were you on January 12th?
Briggs: January 12th?
Detective: Yeah. It was a Wednesday.
Briggs: I can't remember.
Detective: I can. You were in Brooklyn.
Briggs: Oh, no, I wasn't. You're wrong.
Detective: Oh, yes, you were.
Briggs: Oh, no, I wasn't.
Detective: You were!
Briggs: I was in prison in January. Remember?
Detective: Oh, yeah.

Questions

Where were you at one o'clock?	I was at home.
five after two?	school.
ten after three?	work.
a quarter after four?	the laundry.
five-thirty?	the movies.
twenty-five to six?	the barber.
twenty to seven?	the supermarket.
a quarter to eight?	the bank.

Questions

When were you in New York?	I was there in January.
Europe?	February.
Mexico?	March.
Brazil?	April.
Colombia?	May.
California?	June.
Italy?	July.
Japan?	August.
	September.
	October.
	November.
	December.

Exercise 1

Look at this example:
I/here/two o'clock
I was here at two o'clock.

1 He/Italy/July
2 They/home/Sunday
3 You/here/one o'clock
4 She/school/yesterday
5 It/cold/January
6 We/Rio/Wednesday

Exercise 2

Look at this example:
You/New York/February?
Were you in New York in February?

1 he/Oregon/November?
2 it/hot/June?
3 they/at work/five-thirty?
4 she/home/Thursday?
5 you/there/four o'clock
6 they/China/December?

42 Vacations

Diane: Hi, Joe. Where were you last month?

Joe: Oh, hi, Diane. Well, I was on vacation.

Diane: Really? But you were on vacation in January.

Joe: Yes, I was in Bermuda in January.

Diane: Where were you last month?

Joe: I was in Florida.

Diane: Florida! What was it like?

Joe: Fantastic! The weather was beautiful. The ocean was warm.

Diane: What was the hotel like?

Joe: Excellent! There was a swimming pool and a private beach. There were three restaurants. There were tennis courts and a golf course.

Diane: What were the people like?

Joe: They were very friendly.

Diane: Was your wife with you?

Joe: Oh, she wasn't with me.

Diane: Huh? Why not?

Joe: She never takes her vacation with me. She was in Guadeloupe.

Diane: Well, what about your children? Were they with you?

Joe: No, they weren't. They were with their grandparents.

HOTEL ROYAL ☆☆☆
☆ A SWIMMING POOL!
☆ THREE RESTAURANTS!
☆ A PRIVATE BEACH!
☆ TWO BARS!
☆ A DISCOTHEQUE!
☆ TWO ORCHESTRAS!
☆ A CASINO!
☆ FOUR TENNIS COURTS!

Exercise 1

There was a swimming pool.
There were three restaurants.
Now you write six other sentences.

Exercise 2

weather
What was the weather *like?*

restaurants
What were the restaurants *like?*

1 service
2 shops
3 food
4 beaches
5 hotel
6 people

43 Everyday conversation

W: Can I exchange this sweater, please?
X: Why? What's wrong with it?
W: Well, it's the wrong size.
X: Is it too big or too small?
W: It's too small for me.
X: What size are you?
W: I'm not sure.
X: You're probably a large. This one's the right size, I think.

sweater
T-shirt
blouse
shirt
nightgown
bathrobe

large
extra large
small
medium

Y: I'd like some strawberry ice cream, please.
Z: A single or a double scoop?
Y: A single scoop, please. A double's too much for me.
Z: In a cup or a cone?
Y: A cone.
Z: O.K. That's 85¢. Please pay the cashier.

strawberry
vanilla
chocolate
peach
coffee
pistachio
raspberry
honey

A: Excuse me!
B: Yes?
A: I think this change is wrong.
B: Are you sure? Let me see. Oh, yes, I am sorry. You need another dime.
A: Yes, that's right.
B: I'm terribly sorry. I'm so busy here . . .
A: That's O.K. Don't worry about it.

dime (10¢)
penny (1¢)
nickel (5¢)
quarter (25¢)
half dollar (50¢)
dollar (1.00)

C: I think the food here is excellent.
D: Really? I don't think so.
C: Why not?
D: It's too spicy for me. I prefer French food.

spicy
hot
rich
heavy
fattening

French
Turkish
German
Spanish
Chinese
Italian
Japanese
Brazilian

44 Return from space

Phil Strongarm, the astronaut, is talking about his journey to the moon. Walter Concrete, the TV news reporter, is interviewing Phil.

Walter: Well, Phil, welcome back to earth.
Phil: Thanks, Walter.
Walter: Did you have any problems on the trip into space?
Phil: We didn't have any serious problems, but it certainly wasn't a picnic.
Walter: What do you mean?
Phil: We didn't have a bath or shave for two weeks.
Walter: Really?
Phil: Yes. It wasn't very comfortable.
Walter: What about food? Was that a problem?
Phil: Well, we didn't have any normal food.
Walter: What did you have?
Phil: We had some food tablets and other kinds of food in tubes.
Walter: Are you going to the moon again?
Phil: I hope so. It was uncomfortable and difficult but it was wonderful.

Questions
Who's Phil Strongarm?
What's Phil talking about?
Who's interviewing him?
Were they comfortable or uncomfortable?
Did they have any normal food?
What did they have?
Is Phil going to the moon again?
Was it wonderful?

Exercise 1

I/breakfast/eight o'clock
I had breakfast at eight o'clock.

1 You/coffee/eleven o'clock
2 He/lunch/12:30
3 She/a snack/3:30
4 They/dinner/eight o'clock
5 We/supper/nine o'clock

Exercise 2

they/a vacation/last year?
Did they have a vacation last year?

1 he/a haircut/last week?
2 you/a good time/last night?
3 she/a birthday/last month?
4 they/a party/last weekend?
5 you/an appointment/this morning?

Exercise 3

We/a lesson/Sunday
We didn't have a lesson on Sunday.

1 He/a date/Saturday
2 She/a haircut/Monday
3 We/a drink/Tuesday
4 I/a party/Thursday
5 He/a good time/Friday

45 Did you get everything?

Joe Carter goes downtown every Saturday afternoon. He went downtown last Saturday. He usually has a drink in a bar with his friends. Last Saturday he had four or five drinks. After he leaves the bar, he usually goes to the supermarket and gets the food for the week. He got the food last Saturday. He usually comes home by bus. But last Saturday he came home by taxi.

Questions

Does he usually go downtown on
 Saturday?
What about last Saturday?
Does he meet his friends sometimes?
What about last Saturday?
Does he usually have a drink?
What about last Saturday?
Does he usually buy the food for the
 whole week?
What about last Saturday?
Does he usually come home by bus?
What about last Saturday?

Sue Carter: Joe, is that you?
Joe Carter: Yes, Sue. I'm back.
Sue: Did you come home by
 taxi?
Joe: Yes, I did. The bags were
 very heavy.
Sue: Did you get everything?
Joe: Yes. I got everything . . .
 nearly everything.
Sue: Nearly everything?
Joe: Well, I went to the butcher,
 but they didn't have any steak.
Sue: They didn't have any
 steak?
Joe: No, so I got some
 hamburgers.
Sue: Did you go to the bakery?
Joe: Yes, but I didn't get any
 bread.
Sue: You didn't get any bread?
Joe: Well, no, they didn't have
 any bread. So I got some rolls.
Sue: How many rolls did you
 get?
Joe: Uh, I can't remember.
Sue: Joe?
Joe: Yes?
Sue: Did you go to the bar again?
Joe: Uh . . . well . . .
Sue: How many drinks did you
 have?
Joe: Only four or five . . . small
 ones.

Exercise 1

They had some hamburgers.
They didn't have any steak.
Did they have any chicken?
1 He came home by taxi.
 . . . by car.
 . . . by bus?
2 He went to the butcher.
 . . . drugstore.
 . . . bakery?
3 He got some rolls.
 . . . bread.
 . . . hamburgers?

Exercise 2

Answer these questions with "Yes, I did"
or "No, I didn't."
1 Did you go downtown last Saturday?
 . . .
2 Did you get anything? . . .
3 Did you come home by bus? . . .
4 Did you have any drinks yesterday?
 . . .

46 In the office

Jane: Hello, Gloria.
Gloria: Hi, Jane. Did you enjoy lunch?
Jane: Yes, I did. Did you finish those reports?
Gloria: Yes, I typed them. They're on your desk.
Jane: Did you photocopy them?
Gloria: Yes, two copies for each report. And I mailed the letters too.
Jane: Good. Thank you.
Gloria: You're welcome. Oh, Mr. Thompson dropped by to see you.
Jane: Mr. Thompson? Did he call for an appointment first?
Gloria: No, he didn't.
Jane: What time did he arrive?
Gloria: About two o'clock. But he only waited about five minutes.
Jane: That's strange. What did he want?
Gloria: He probably wanted some free advice.
Jane: Did anybody telephone?
Gloria: No, nobody.
Jane: Oh, no!
Gloria: What's the matter?
Jane: You mailed the letters . . .
Gloria: Yes, of course.
Jane: But I didn't sign them!
Gloria: I signed them . . . with my name.
Jane: Next time, please wait for me to sign them.

Exercise

Who typed the reports?
Gloria *typed the reports.*
Jane *didn't type the reports.*
Did Mr. Thompson *type the reports?*

1 Who mailed the letters?
  Gloria . . . .
  Jane . . . .
  . . . Mr. Thompson . . . ?

2 Who dropped by?
  Mr. Thompson . . . .
  Jane . . . .
  . . . Gloria . . . ?

3 Who wanted advice?
  Mr. Thompson . . . .
  Gloria . . . .
  . . . Jane . . . ?

47 The Legend of Willy the Kid

WILLY THE KID ARRIVED IN DODGE CITY ONE EVENING.

HE WALKED INTO THE SALOON, AND LOOKED SLOWLY ROUND THE ROOM.

EVERYBODY WAS AFRAID. WILLY HAD TWO GUNS.

THE SHERIFF WAS IN HIS OFFICE. HE WAS ASLEEP.

WILLY THE KID'S IN TOWN

THE SALOON BARMAN RUSHED INTO THE SHERIFF'S OFFICE.

THE SHERIFF HURRIED TO THE SALOON.

GIVE ME YOUR GUNS, WILLY.

THIS TOWN IS TOO SMALL FOR BOTH OF US.

THE SHERIFF SHOUTED TO WILLY.

WILLY REPLIED CALMLY.

THEY WALKED INTO THE STREET. THE SHERIFF WAITED. WILLY MOVED HIS HAND TOWARDS HIS GUN...

THE SHERIFF PULLED OUT HIS GUN. HE FIRED TWICE.

THE FIRST BULLET MISSED WILLY. THE SECOND KILLED HIM.

TWO COWBOYS CARRIED WILLY AWAY. THAT WAS THE END OF WILLY THE KID.

Exercise

1 He walked into the saloon.
He didn't . . . into the office.
Did he . . . into the bank?
2 They carried Willy away.
They . . . carry the sheriff away.
. . . they carry the barman away?

48 Foreign vacations

Maria's a student at New York University. She studies Spanish, and she goes to Mexico every summer. She lies in the sun, drinks a lot of beer, and eats a lot of delicious Mexican food. She always flies to Mexico by AeroMexico.

Questions

1 Is Maria a student?
2 Does she study sociology and French?
3 Ask, "What?"
4 Does she go to Brazil every summer?
5 Ask, "Where?"
6 What does she do in Mexico?
7 How does she get there?

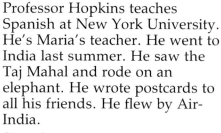

Professor Hopkins teaches Spanish at New York University. He's Maria's teacher. He went to India last summer. He saw the Taj Mahal and rode on an elephant. He wrote postcards to all his friends. He flew by Air-India.

Questions

1 What does Professor Hopkins teach?
2 Where did he go last summer?
3 What did he see?
4 What did he ride on?
5 Who did he write to?
6 Did he fly by Air-India or TWA?

Maria's parents went to Italy last year. They toured the whole country by bus. They saw a lot of interesting places. They ate spaghetti in Rome, drank coffee in Venice, and took a lot of photographs. The sun shone every day. They flew to Italy by Alitalia.

Questions

1 Where did Maria's parents go?
2 How did they tour the whole country?
3 What did they eat?
4 What did they drink?
5 How many photographs did they take?
6 What was the weather like?
7 Did they go to Italy by plane or by boat?

Paulo's from Brazil. He hitch-hiked around the United States last summer. He stayed there for a month. Of course he ate hamburgers and drank Coca-Cola. He met a lot of interesting people. He bought a lot of souvenirs and took them back to Brazil. He flew there by Varig.

Questions

1 What did Paulo do last summer?
2 How long did he stay?
3 What did he eat?
4 What did he drink?
5 Who did he meet?
6 What did he buy?
7 What did he do with his souvenirs?
8 Did he have a good time or a bad time?

Exercise

a Anne/go/Spain
b He/not/Spain
c you/Spain?

a Anne *went to* Spain.
b He *didn't go to* Spain.
c *Did* you *go to* Spain?

a They/eat/spaghetti
b He/not/spaghetti
c you/spaghetti?

a They/drink/coffee
b She/not/coffee
c you/coffee?

a He/see/Taj Mahal
b She/not/TajMahal
c you/Taj Mahal?

a He/buy/records
b They/not/records
c you/records?

Look at this

have	had
come	came
go	went
get	got
see	saw
eat	ate
drink	drank
take	took
fly	flew
shine	shone
meet	met
write	wrote
ride	rode
buy	bought
bring	brought

49 Survivors

Bill Craig and Chris Alonso are test pilots. Last year their plane crashed in the Pacific Ocean. They were in a rubber lifeboat for four weeks.

They didn't have much water, and they didn't have many things to eat.

They had a few bananas and a little brandy from their plane. They caught a lot of fish.

They had only a little chocolate. They had only a few crackers and a few apples. They lost a lot of weight.

After four weeks they got lucky. They saw a ship and it rescued them. They wrote a book about their experience. It's called *Survivors*.

Questions

What are their names?
What do they do?
Did their plane crash?
Ask, "When?"
Ask, "Where?"
How many weeks were they in a lifeboat?
How much water did they have?
Did they have many bananas?
Did they have much brandy?
Did they catch any fish?
Ask, "How many?"
How much chocolate did they have?
How many crackers did they have?
How many apples did they have?
What happened after four weeks?
What did they write?

Exercise 1

chocolate

A Did they have any chocolate?
B Yes, they did. But they didn't have much.

A How much chocolate did they have?
B They had only a little.

water

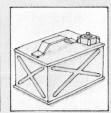
gas

brandy

Exercise 2

matches

A Did they have any matches?
B Yes, they did. But they didn't have many.

A How many matches did they have?
B They had only a few.

crackers

apples

bananas

Exercise 3

He doesn't have *much* money.
He has only *a little* money.

1 He doesn't have . . . friends.
2 He has only . . . friends.
3 He doesn't have . . . wine.
4 He has only . . . wine.

She doesn't have *many* dollars.
She has only *a few* dollars.

5 She didn't have . . . Swiss francs.
6 She had only . . . French francs.
7 There isn't . . . gas.
8 We have only . . . gas.

50 Sleeping Beauty

Cathy: Good morning, Dennis.
Dennis: Hi, Cathy.
Cathy: Gee, I'm tired this morning.
Dennis: You are? Why?
Cathy: Well, I went to the ballet last night.
Dennis: You did? What did you see?
Cathy: I saw "Sleeping Beauty."
Dennis: Who was in it?
Cathy: Heather Kirkland and Rudolf Barishnev. And there was a new dancer — Lourdes Lopez.
Dennis: Was Heather Kirkland good?
Cathy: She usually dances well, but last night she danced badly.
Dennis: Really? But Barishnev was good, of course . . .
Cathy: Well . . . last night he didn't do very well.
Dennis: Incredible! But what about Lourdes Lopez?
Cathy: She's a very good dancer. She danced beautifully.
Dennis: New dancers always work hard. They're never careless.
Cathy: Oh, do you like ballet too?
Dennis: Not really. I prefer disco dancing.

Questions

What are their names?
Who's tired?
Ask, "Why?"
Which ballet did she see?
Who was in it?
How does Heather Kirkland usually dance?
How did she dance last night?
How did Barishnev do last night?
How did Lourdes Lopez dance?
Do new dancers always work hard?
Are they ever careless?
Does Dennis like the ballet too?

Exercise 1

He's a good dancer.
He usually dances well.

1 They're beautiful dancers.
2 She's a careless writer.
3 He's a hard worker.
4 He's a bad football player.
5 They're good drivers.

Exercise 2

He usually dances well, *but yesterday he danced badly.*

1 She usually writes carefully, ...
2 She usually types slowly, ...
3 They usually sing badly, ...
4 He usually works fast, ...
5 He usually answers carelessly, ...

51 Everyday conversation

E: Excuse me. I lost my glasses this morning.
F: Where did you lose them?
E: On the fifth floor — in the furniture department.
F: Well, you're lucky. A salesman found them about an hour ago.
E: Thank goodness! I was really worried.
F: Here they are. He gave them to me a few minutes ago.
E: Yes. Those are mine. Thank you so much.

glasses
packages
umbrella
wallet
shopping bags
camera

a few minutes ago
about an hour ago
at lunchtime
15 minutes ago
about half an hour ago

G: What did you do last weekend?
H: I went to San Francisco.
G: Really? How did you go?
H: I went by car.
G: How long did it take?
H: It took about two hours.
G: Why did you go there?
H: I had nothing else to do.

last weekend
last Saturday
last night

by car
by taxi
by train
by bus

I: Hi, Bill. I thought you were in Atlantic City.
J: I was. I drove there on Friday.
I: And?
J: And I came back on Saturday morning.
I: Why did you come back so soon?
J: Well, I went to a casino and spent all my money.
I: How did you do that?
J: Well, I won a little at first, and then I lost everything.

Atlantic City
Las Vegas
Reno
San Juan
Santo Domingo

Saturday morning
Sunday evening
Monday night
Tuesday afternoon
this morning

K: Would you like a cigarette?
L: No, thanks. I'm trying to stop.
K: Oh, come on. Have one.
L: No, really. I have a terrible cough and a sore throat.

stop
give it up
give up smoking
quit

52 The Six O'Clock News

Good evening. And here's the Six O'Clock News from Washington with J. C. Kennedy and Warren Wolf.

Last night there was an earthquake in Mandanga. The earthquake destroyed the Central Bank. Many buildings fell down. The Mandangan army is in the capital. They are helping survivors. The International Red Cross sent planes with food and medicine to the area this morning.

Questions

What happened in Mandanga?
Ask, "When?"
Did the earthquake destroy the airport?
Ask, "What?"
How many buildings fell down?
Where is the army?
What are they doing?
What did the Red Cross do?
Ask, "When?"

The Virginia police are looking for two climbers in the Blue Ridge Mountains. The climbers left yesterday morning to climb Mount Blue. It began to snow heavily yesterday afternoon. The police sent out a search party last night. They spent the night on the mountain, but they didn't find the climbers.

Questions

How many climbers are the police looking for?
Ask, "Where?"
When did they leave?
What did they want to climb?
Did it rain or did it snow?
Who sent out a search party?
Ask, "When?"
Did they spend the night in a hotel?
Ask, "Where?"
Did they find the climbers?

Yesterday, Nancy Burns, the wife of Washington, D.C., mayor Barry Burns, opened a new rehabilitation center in the D.C. Hospital. She met all the doctors and nurses, and spoke to the first patients. Mrs. Burns does a lot of work with the handicapped.

Questions

Who opened a new rehabilitation center?
Ask, "When?"
Ask, "Where?"
Who did she meet?
Who did she speak to?
Who does she do a lot of work with?

. . . and next, football. This afternoon at D.C. Stadium, the Washington Redskins played the Dallas Cowboys. Dallas lost twenty-one to fourteen. The Dallas kicker broke his leg. The Redskins played very well. Quarterback Joe Kilmer scored three touchdowns for the Redskins.

Questions

Who did the Washington Redskins play?
Ask, "Where?"
Did they win or did they lose?
Who broke his leg?
Which team played well?
What did quarterback Joe Kilmer do?

53 Howard Hughes 1905–1976
Biography of a Billionaire

December 24, 1905 Howard Hughes was born in Houston, Texas.

1912 He started school.

1924 His father died. He left school. He inherited $750,000. He became director of his father's oil-drilling company.

1925 He married Ella Rice.

1927 He went to Hollywood.

1928 He produced a movie. He divorced Ella Rice.

1930 He directed the movie *Hell's Angels*.

1933 He worked as an airline pilot. (He changed his name.)

1935 He built a plane. He broke the world air-speed record. (He flew at 352 miles per hour.)

1937 President Roosevelt gave him a special aviation award.

1938 He flew around the world in 91 hours (a new world record).

1942 He designed and manufactured war planes.

1943 He discovered Jane Russell. He directed *The Outlaw*. She became a famous movie star.

1947 He started TWA (Trans World Airlines). He crashed a new war plane. He nearly died. In the hospital, he designed a new bed. He flew a new 700-seat passenger plane.

1948 He bought RKO Pictures — a Hollywood movie studio.

1954 He sold RKO.

1957 He sold TWA for $546,000,000. He married actress Jean Peters.

1958 He retired from public life.

1966 He went to Las Vegas. He bought a lot of gambling casinos, nightclubs, and hotels. (He didn't smoke, drink, or gamble.)

1971 He divorced Jean Peters.

1972 He gave $100,000 to President Nixon for the presidential campaign.

April 5, 1976 Howard Hughes died in Acapulco. He left $2,000,000,000.

54 The boss and the secretary

George Goodridge: Well, Ms. Bradley. This is a change! I usually have water with my meals, you know.

Jennifer Bradley: Yes, Mr. Goodridge, but tonight we're having champagne!

GG: Please don't call me Mr. Goodridge. My friends always call me George.

JB: All right, George. And tonight we're having filet mignon.

GG: Isn't it wonderful? I normally have franks and beans on Mondays. You see, my mother doesn't like restaurants.

JB: Oh, you live with your mother? What's she doing now?

GG: Oh, she's watching television. Uh, what perfume are you wearing, Ms. Bradley?

JB: Please call me Jennifer. I'm wearing "Night of Passion."

GG: It's lovely.

JB: I don't always wear it, but this is a special occasion.

GG: Of course it is. I never come to restaurants like this. Uh, Jennifer, I want to ask you a question. It's very important.

JB: Oh, George, I'm enjoying this evening so much. You can ask me anything.

GG: Well, it's difficult . . .

JB: Please ask me.

GG: O.K. You know we have a lot of work at the office.

JB: Yes?

GG: Well, can you work on Saturdays until we finish it?

JB: What? Is that the important question? Why didn't you ask me in the office?

GG: But, Jennifer . . .

JB: You can call me Ms. Bradley. Goodnight, Mr. Goodridge.

Questions

1 What's he drinking tonight?
2 What does he usually drink?
3 What's he eating tonight?
4 What does he usually eat on Mondays?
5 Is Ms. Bradley wearing perfume tonight?
6 Does she always wear perfume?

Exercise

He usually drinks water.
tonight/champagne
But tonight he's drinking champagne.

1 He usually eats eggs.
   tonight/steak
2 She usually drinks beer.
   tonight/wine
3 He usually smokes cigars.
   tonight/cigarettes
4 She usually eats at home.
   tonight/in a restaurant

55 An accident

Two cars were going down Second Street in Lawrence, Kansas. A middle-aged woman was driving a Chevrolet. Right behind her a teenage student was driving an old Ford. The woman was driving slowly and carefully. The student wasn't driving carefully. He was worrying about his courses in school. He was doing badly in Spanish and Physics. He was worrying about the final exams, so he wasn't paying attention to the road. . . . The traffic light was green. A dog was sitting on the corner near the traffic light. A cat was sitting on the opposite corner.

The dog was thinking about a bone.

Suddenly the dog saw the cat.

It ran across the road.

The woman saw the dog.

She quickly put her foot on the brakes.

The Ford crashed into the Chevrolet.

A girl saw the accident.

She ran to a telephone booth.

The police and an ambulance came immediately.

56 An investigation

Last night at 9:18 p.m., Mr. Scott Shaw, a high school principal, was walking from his office to his car when he was attacked from behind. The attacker hit the principal on the head. The police think the attacker was a student. They are going to question every student in the school — both male and female.

Questions

When did it happen?
What time did it happen?
Where was the principal going?
Where was he coming from?
Did the attacker hit him?
Where did the attacker hit him?
What do the police think?
What are they going to do?

A policeman questioned the victim at the hospital last night:

Policeman: What can you remember about the attack, Mr. Shaw?

Mr. Shaw: Well, I was working late last night.

Policeman: What time did you leave your office?

Mr. Shaw: At about a quarter after nine.

Policeman: Are you sure?

Mr. Shaw: Yes, I am. I looked at my watch.

Policeman: What did you do then?

Mr. Shaw: Well, I locked the office door, and I was walking to the parking lot when somebody hit me on the head.

Policeman: Did you see the attacker?

Mr. Shaw: No. He was wearing a mask over his face.

Policeman: He? Oh, so it was a man!

Mr. Shaw: Well, I'm not really sure. No . . . no, I don't know.

Policeman: Tell me, Mr. Shaw, how did you break your leg?

Mr. Shaw: Well, when they were putting me into the ambulance, they dropped me!

Questions

Where's the victim now?
What's he doing?
What's the policeman doing?
What was Mr. Shaw doing at 9 p.m. yesterday?
What time did he leave his office?
Is he sure?
Ask, "Why?"
What did he lock?
When did the attacker hit him?
Did he see the attacker?
Ask, "Why not?"
Was the attacker a man or a woman?
Did Mr. Shaw break his arm?
Ask, "What?"
Ask, "When?"

57 A photo album

Rosa Sanchez is 26 years old. She's a music teacher. She's teaching a class now.

Rosa: Christopher, can you read music?

Christopher: Yes, Mrs. Sanchez, I can. I could read music when I was ten.

Rosa: You could? That's wonderful!

Christopher: Mrs. Sanchez, could you read music when you were ten?

Rosa: Well, I could read music when I was eight.

Christopher: Really? Could you write music when you were eight?

Rosa: No, Christopher. Of course I couldn't.

Christopher: Mozart could.

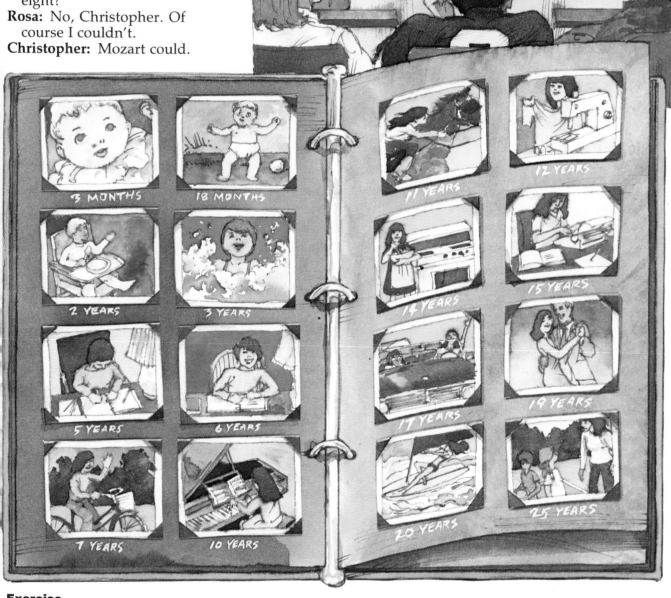

Exercise

When Rosa was ten, she could play the piano, and she could ride a bike. But she couldn't speak French, and she couldn't sew.

Now write ten sentences about yourself:
When I was ten, I could read.
When I was ten, I couldn't speak English.

58 A spy story

M: This is a very important mission, 005.

005: What do I have to do?

M: You have to go to Moscow on the next flight.

005: Moscow! I have a good friend there . . . a woman . . .

M: Yes, we know that. But you can't visit her!

005: Where do I have to stay?

M: You have to go directly to the Airport Hotel, stay in your room, and wait for instructions.

005: Which passport do I have to use?

M: Your Swiss passport. And you have to speak German all the time. They can't discover your real nationality.

005: Do I have to take my gun?

M: No, you can't take your gun . . . but take a lot of warm clothes. Good luck, 005!

Questions

Is it an important mission?
Does he have to go to Moscow?
Ask, "When?" Ask, "How?"
Who can't he visit in Moscow?
Does he have to stay in a hotel?
Ask, "Which hotel?"
Does he have to stay in his room?
What does he have to wait for?
Which passport does he have to use?
Does he have to speak English?
Ask, "What?" Ask, "Why?"
Does he have to take his gun?
What does he have to take with him?

X: Listen carefully, Olga. You have to check into the Airport Hotel tonight.

Olga: Do I need to reserve a room?

X: No, you don't. We made a reservation for you . . . next to the English agent's room.

Olga: Do I have to stay in my room?

X: No, you don't, but you have to stay in the hotel.

Olga: Do I have to . . . be nice to him?

X: No, you don't. But you need to find out why he's here.

Olga: Do I have to contact you every day?

X: No, no, you can't! It's too dangerous for you.

Olga: Why?

X: Because 005 is a very dangerous man.

Olga: Don't worry, X. I'm a very dangerous woman!

Questions

Does she have to check into the hotel tonight?
Does she need to reserve a room?
Does she have to stay in her room?
Where does she have to stay?
Does she have to be nice to 005?
What does she need to find out?
Does she need to contact X every day?
Ask, "Why not?"

Exercise

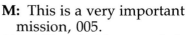

I'm on a diet, so I can't eat bread.
I can't drink beer.
I can't go everywhere by car.

I'm a millionaire, so I don't have to work.
I don't have to save money.
I don't have to worry about inflation.

Write six true sentences.
Begin
I can't . . . .
I don't have to . . . .

59 Everyday conversation

M: Hello?
N: Hello. Is Linda Green there, please?
M: Who's calling, please?
N: Tom Piper.
M: Hold on a minute. I'll see.
N: Thanks.
M: Uh, hello. I'm sorry, but Linda's out.
N: Oh. When do you expect her back?
M: I'm not sure.
N: Could you take a message?
M: Yes, of course.

Hold on a minute.
Just a minute, please.
I'll see if she's in.
Would you hold on, please?
Wait a minute, please.

out
not at her desk
not here
in a meeting
busy

O: Directory Assistance. May I help you?
P: Yes. I'd like the number of Sophie Shoemaker. 492 Cole Road, Topeka.
O: Just a moment, please . . . Area code (913) 682-1140.
P: Can I dial direct for a collect call?
O: Yes, you can. Just dial 0 and the number.
P: Thanks.
O: You're welcome . . . have a nice day.

Topeka
Los Angeles
Portland
Galveston
Des Moines

(913)
(213)
(503)
(713)
(515)

Q: Hello. Orange Cabs.
R: I'd like a taxi, please.
Q: What's your name?
R: Ed Rios.
Q: What's your address?
R: 99 Jane Street.
Q: Is that a house or an apartment?
R: An apartment. 14G.
Q: Where are you going?
R: To Lincoln Center.
Q: O.K. Cab number 1502 in ten minutes.
R: Thanks.

Lincoln Center
Port Authority Bus Terminal
Grand Central Station
Roosevelt Hospital
Kennedy Airport

S: Operator.
T: Hello. Can I dial direct to Rio de Janeiro, Brazil, from New York?
S: Yes. First you dial the international code number 011.
T: What do I do next?
S: Next you dial the country code and the city code. Brazil is 55, and Rio is 21.
T: And then?
S: Then you dial the local telephone number.
T: Oh, that's easy.

Rio de Janeiro, Brazil
Tokyo, Japan
Athens, Greece
Maracaibo, Venezuela

55/21
81/3
30/1
58/61

60 Another personal letter

Pensión San Jose
Hamburgo 243
Zona Rosa
Mexico 5, D.F.
August 21st

Dear John,
    Last weekend I went on a trip to Merida - a lovely city on the Yucatán Peninsula. I went with some students in my class. First we visited Uxmal, an old Mayan City about 50 miles south of Merida. Then we climbed the old Pyramid of the Magician. It was very interesting - 118 steps to the top of the Pyramid! We saw the Governor's Palace and the House of Pigeons. After lunch we sat in the sun for an hour and walked around. I met a very interesting Mexican there. I didn't practice my Spanish because he spoke English all the time.
    Did you have a nice weekend?
I miss you a lot.   Love, Mary

Dear	Joe,
	Anne,
	Dad,
	Mom,

Last	Monday	I went	on a trip	to	Cambridge, Massachusetts.	I went with
	night		*on a bus tour*		*New Haven, Connecticut.*	
	weekend		*on vacation*		*Princeton, New Jersey.*	

my girlfriend.	I got up	early	and met	her	at the	station.
some friends.		*at seven o'clock*		*them*		*school.*
my boyfriend.		*late*		*him*		*bus station.*

In the morning we visited	Harvard.	We saw the	stadium	and the	downtown area.
	Yale.		*dormitories*		*classroom buildings.*
	Princeton.		*gymnasium*		*library.*

It was very	interesting	We had lunch in a	restaurant,	and I drank a lot of	soda.
	beautiful.		*coffee shop,*		*beer.*
	dull.		*cafeteria,*		*wine.*

In the afternoon we sat	in a garden	and walked	through the park.	I met a very	interesting
	by the river		*around the campus.*		*handsome*
	in the park		*around town.*		*beautiful*

graduate student	with	brown eyes.	I didn't practice my English because	he	spoke	Spanish.
Californian		*a beard.*		*she*		*Arabic.*
man/woman		*long hair.*				*Japanese.*

| Did you have a | nice weekend? | I miss you a lot. |
| | *good week?* | |

    Love,

61 On the moon

The *Eagle* has landed on the moon! Astronaut Phil Strongarm is speaking to Mission Control in Houston.

Mission Control: Hello, Phil. Can you hear me?

Strongarm: Yes, I can hear you clearly.

Mission Control: What are you going to do next?

Strongarm: I'm going to open the door.

Mission Control: Hello, Phil. What are you doing now?

Strongarm: I'm opening the door.

Mission Control: Phil! Have you opened the door?

Strongarm: Yes, I've opened it! I can see the moon, and it's fantastic!

Exercise

1 What's he going to do?
He's going to climb down the ladder.

What's he doing?
He's climb*ing* down the ladder.

What has he done?
He's climb*ed* down the ladder.

2 What's he going to do?
He's going to raise the flag.

. . . . ?
. . . .

. . . . ?
. . . .

3 What's he going to do?
He's going to close the door.

. . . . ?
. . . .

. . . . ?
. . . .

62 Where's he gone?

Nancy: Janet, what's the matter?

Janet: It's my husband. He's gone!

Nancy: Gone? Where's he gone?

Janet: He's gone to Acapulco.

Nancy: Oh, Janet. You poor thing. I'm so sorry. Has he gone with . . . with another woman?

Janet: What? Of course not. He hasn't gone with another woman. He's gone there on business.

Nancy: When's he coming back?

Janet: Tomorrow.

Nancy: I don't understand. Why are you crying?

Janet: I miss him.

Nancy: Look, Janet, there's a new movie at the theater downtown . . . "Star Wars—Five."

Janet: Yes?

Nancy: Well, stop crying and let's go and see it!

Paul: Hey, Bill, can you lend me $10?

Bill: Sorry, I can't. I haven't been to the bank today.

Paul: Oh, I haven't been there either, and I need some money. We could go now.

Bill: No, the bank's closed now. It's three o'clock. Why don't you ask Pete?

Paul: Has he been to the bank?

Bill: He probably has. He always goes to the bank on Mondays.

Exercise

He's *been to the* bank.

She . . . supermarket.

They . . . church.

He . . . barber.

She's *gone to* Paris.

They . . . London.

He . . . hospital.

He . . . on business.

63 Everyday conversation

U: Oh, no!
V: What's wrong?
U: I can't find my pen.
V: Really? Ha ha ha.
U: You don't have to laugh. It isn't funny.
V: Oh, yes, it is.
U: It is? I don't understand the joke.
V: Well, you have to look carefully.
U: I've looked everywhere.
V: No, you haven't. Look behind your ear.
U: Oh.

pen
pencil
address book
checkbook

behind your ear
in your hand
in your pocket
on your desk
under your elbow

W: Are you a foreigner?
X: What?
W: ARE-YOU-A-FOREIGNER?
X: You don't have to shout. I'm not deaf.
W: Oh, I'm sorry.
X: That's O.K. I just didn't understand the word *foreigner*. What does it mean?

foreigner
tourist
student
teacher

Y: Watch out! I've just washed the floor.
Z: No, you haven't.
Y: Yes, I have.
Z: Well, you haven't done a good job. Look over there. You've missed a spot.
Y: You're right. Here's the mop.

floor
walls
windows
mirrors

mop
sponge
rag
bucket

A: I'm so bored.
B: Well, do something.
A: What, for example?
B: Wash your hair.
A: I've already washed it.
B: Call your friend Susan.
A: I've already talked to her today.
B: Clean your room.
A: I've already cleaned it.
B: Then do the dishes.
A: Haven't you done them yet?
B: No, I haven't.
A: Oh, all right.

wash/hair
finish/homework
iron/clothes
brush/teeth
do/homework

64 City and country

Chris: Jeff! I've got a new job! I'm going to live in New York.
Jeff: You are? I lived in New York five years ago.
Chris: Did you like it?
Jeff: Not very much.
Chris: Why not?
Jeff: Well, there were too many people, and there was too much noise.
Chris: I love crowds and noise!
Jeff: Well, I don't. And I don't like pollution.
Chris: What do you mean?
Jeff: There isn't enough fresh air in New York.
Chris: But you can go to concerts and the ballet and Broadway and —
Jeff: Who has enough money for all that? And the rents are very high.
Chris: Why is that?
Jeff: Because there aren't enough apartments.
Chris: Well, I still prefer big cities.
Jeff: But why?
Chris: I was born in a small town. It was too quiet and too dull.
Jeff: You were lucky.
Chris: I don't think so. There wasn't much to do. That's why young people go to New York.
Jeff: But New York's too expensive for young people.
Chris: But they still go. They want excitement.
Jeff: Well, I don't want excitement. I just want a quiet life, that's all.

Exercise

In New York

There's too much noise.
There isn't enough fresh air.
There are too many people.
There aren't enough apartments.

In the world

1 . . . pollution.
2 . . . oil.
3 . . . people.
4 . . . doctors.

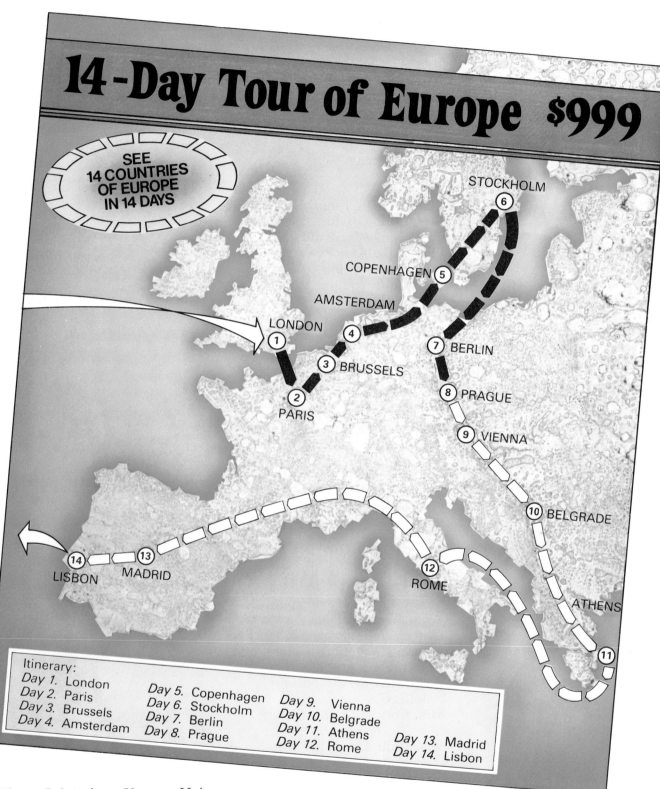

14-Day Tour of Europe $999

SEE 14 COUNTRIES OF EUROPE IN 14 DAYS

STOCKHOLM (6)

COPENHAGEN (5)

AMSTERDAM

LONDON (1) (4)

(3) BRUSSELS

(7) BERLIN

(2) (8) PRAGUE

PARIS (9) VIENNA

(10) BELGRADE

(14) (13) (12) (11)

LISBON MADRID ROME ATHENS

Itinerary:
Day 1. London
Day 2. Paris
Day 3. Brussels
Day 4. Amsterdam
Day 5. Copenhagen
Day 6. Stockholm
Day 7. Berlin
Day 8. Prague
Day 9. Vienna
Day 10. Belgrade
Day 11. Athens
Day 12. Rome
Day 13. Madrid
Day 14. Lisbon

Elmer Colt is from Kansas. He's on a 14-day tour of Europe. The tour started in London. At the moment he's in Prague. It's the eighth day of the tour. He's already been to seven countries and stayed in the capital cities.

He's never been to Europe before, and he's already seen a lot of new places. He's done a lot of interesting things . . . and the tour hasn't finished yet.

Exercise 1

Elmer's been to London, but he hasn't been to Vienna yet.
Write four sentences about Elmer.

Exercise 2

I've been to Paris, but I haven't been to London yet.
Write four sentences about yourself.

Exercise 3

Answer these questions with Yes, I have/ No, I haven't
1 Have you been to California?
2 Have you been to New York?
3 Have you been to Europe?
4 Have you been to Australia?

66 Elmer calls home

KANSAS

PRAGUE

Elmer: Hello, Mom? Is that you?
Mrs. Colt: Oh, Elmer, yes. How are you? Where are you now?
Elmer: I'm fine. I've just arrived in Prague, Mom.
Mrs. Colt: You haven't sent us any postcards yet.
Elmer: Yes, I have. I've sent one from every city.
Mrs. Colt: Have you been to Paris yet, Elmer?
Elmer: Yes, I have.
Mrs. Colt: Have you been to Vienna yet?
Elmer: No, I haven't. We're going to Vienna tomorrow.

Mrs. Colt: Elmer! Are you still there?
Elmer: Yes, Mom.
Mrs. Colt: How many countries have you seen now?
Elmer: Well, this is the eighth day, so I've already seen eight countries.
Mrs. Colt: Have you spent much money?
Elmer: Well, uh, yes, Mom. I've bought a lot of souvenirs, and I want to buy some more. Can you wire me a thousand dollars?
Mrs. Colt: All right, Elmer.

Mrs. Colt: Elmer, are you listening to me?
Elmer: Sure, Mom.
Mrs. Colt: Have you taken many pictures, Elmer?
Elmer: Yes, I've taken a lot. I've used three rolls of film.
Mrs. Colt: Have you met any nice girls yet?
Elmer: Oh, yes, Mom. There's a girl from Texas on the tour. We've done everything together.
Mrs. Colt: Elmer! Elmer! Are you still there?

Exercise 1

postcards
How many postcards *has he sent?*
He's sent one from every city.

Write questions and answers with:
1 capitals
2 money
3 souvenirs
4 photographs
5 rolls of film

Exercise 2

Have you ever bought a souvenir?
Yes, I have.
No, I haven't.

Answer these questions:
Have you ever seen the Golden Gate Bridge?
Have you ever been to Paris?
Have you ever sent a postcard?
Have you ever spent a lot of money on a trip?
Have you ever met a Texan?
Have you ever taken pictures on a trip?

67 Have you ever . . .?

A: Have you ever studied a language before?
B: Yes, I have.
A: Oh, which one did you study?
B: I studied Spanish in high school.

in high school
in college
in night school
at home

C: Have you ever been to a big wedding?
D: Yes, I have.
C: Whose wedding was it?
D: It was my brother's.

brother's
sister's
cousin's
friend's

E: Have you ever seen a fire?
F: Uh, yes, I have.
E: When did you see it?
F: I saw one in Detroit in 1982.

in 1982
in 1961
in 1959
in 1977

G: Have you ever drunk too much?
H: Yes, I have.
G: Where did you drink too much?
H: I drank too much at my brother's wedding.

at my brother's wedding   at a dinner party
at my friend's party   at a nightclub

I: Have you ever eaten at Alfredo's Restaurant?
J: Yes, I have.
I: When did you eat there?
J: Mary and I ate there two months ago.

at Alfredo's Restaurant
at Burger Queen
at the Hong Kong Restaurant
at the San Diego Hilton

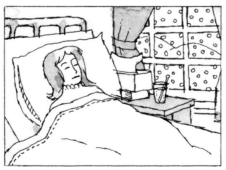

K: Have you ever had the flu?
L: Yes, I have.
K: When did you have it?
L: I had it last winter.

last winter
last spring
last summer
last fall

M: Have you ever broken a bone?
N: Yes, I have.
M: What did you break?
N: I broke my leg.

leg
arm
finger
shoulder

68 Comparisons

Canada (January) −20°C; −4°F

Greenland −32°C; −26°F

Canada's cold, but *Greenland's colder.*

Bermuda 35°C; 95°F

Saudi Arabia 40°C; 104°F

Bermuda's hot, but . . . .

Nancy's older than Billy; so Billy's younger than Nancy.

Make sentences using these words:
tall/short
light/heavy
fat/thin
small/big

Canada's large, but the . . . .

Canada — 10,032,485 square km; 3,849,670 square mi.

U.S.S.R. — 22,402,200 square km
8,649,440 square mi.

Bronx Junior High School
Billy Wilson

English: A+
Math: C
History: C
Geography: B
French: B
Science: D

Bronx Junior High School
Tommy Rivera

English: A
Math: A
History: D
Geography: A
French: C
Science: B

Tommy's better than Billy in Math; so Billy's worse than Tommy.

Make sentences about:
English/History/Geography/French/
Science.

New Orleans, Louisiana
1340 mm rainfall per year
56.7 in.

San Juan, Puerto Rico 1564 mm; 59.2 in.

New Orleans is wet, but . . . .

Mount Everest
8848 m
29,028 ft.

Mount McKinley
6193 m
20,320 ft.

Mount McKinley's high, but . . . .

A car's more expensive than a motorcycle, but a motorcycle's less comfortable than a car.

Make sentences using these words:
comfortable/dangerous/economical/fun/
convenient.

69 A hard life

Jerry Floyd is talking to his grandfather about his new job:

"It's terrible, Grandpa. I have to get up at seven o'clock because I have to catch the bus to work. Because I'm new, I have to make the coffee at work. I have to work hard during the week. I'm only happy on weekends. I don't have to work then."

Questions

Does Jerry have to get up at 6 o'clock?
Does he have to get up at 7 o'clock?
Does he have to catch the train?
Does he have to catch the bus?
Does he have to make the tea?
Does he have to make the coffee?
Does he have to work hard during the week?
Does he have to work hard on weekends?

His grandfather isn't very sympathetic:

"I had to start work when I was 14. I lived in West Virginia, and there wasn't much work. I had to be a coal miner. We had to work twelve hours a day. We didn't have to work on Sundays, but we had to work the other six days of the week.

Questions

Did he have to start work when he was 15, or did he have to start work when he was 14?
Did he live in Pennsylvania, or did he live in West Virginia?
Did he have to be a teacher, or did he have to be a coal miner?
Did he have to work 8 hours a day, or did he have to work 12 hours a day?
Did he have to work 5 days a week, or did he have to work 6 days a week?
Did he have to work on Sundays?

"When I was eighteen, World War I started. I joined the army. I had to wear a uniform, and I had to go to France. A lot of my friends died. We had to obey the officers, and we had to kill people.

Questions

When did World War I start?
How old was he then?
What did he join?
What did he have to wear?
Where did he have to go?
How many of his friends died?
Who did he have to obey?
What did he have to do?

"When I was sixty, I had to go to the hospital because of the dust from the mines. It was the only quiet time in my life. I didn't have to work, and I didn't have to earn money.

Questions

Did he have to go to the hospital?
When did he have to go to the hospital?
Why did he have to go to the hospital?
Did he have to work in the hospital?
Did he have to earn money?

"I retired when I was sixty-five. Nowadays I don't work, and I don't have to get up early. But I have to live on my pension, and life is still difficult. So, Jerry, I don't feel sorry for you."

Questions

Did he retire at 60?
Ask, "When?"
What doesn't he have to do now?
Does he earn money now?
What does he live on?
Is life easy for him now, or is it difficult?
Does he feel sorry for his grandson?

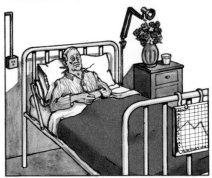

70 Comparisons

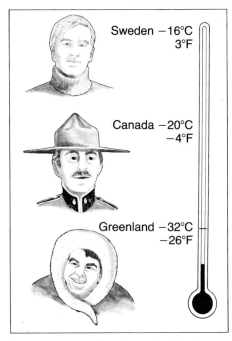

Sweden −16°C
3°F

Canada −20°C
−4°F

Greenland −32°C
−26°F

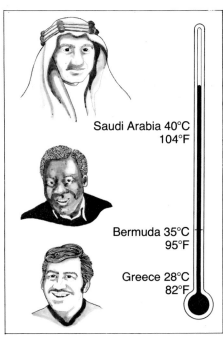

Saudi Arabia 40°C
104°F

Bermuda 35°C
95°F

Greece 28°C
82°F

Mary   Cynthia   Laura

Mary's the tallest.
Cynthia's the shortest.
Make sentences using these words:
light/heavy
old/young
fat/thin
small/big

They're all cold, *but Greenland's the coldest*.

They're all hot, ...

They're all large, ...

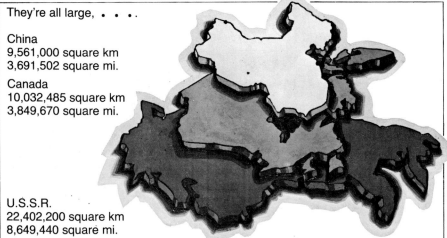

China
9,561,000 square km
3,691,502 square mi.

Canada
10,032,485 square km
3,849,670 square mi.

U.S.S.R.
22,402,200 square km
8,649,440 square mi.

Los Angeles High School Grade Report

	Alan	Robert	Tony
English	A	B+	B
Math	C	D	A
History	B	A	C
Spanish	B	A	A+
Physics	B+	B	A
Music	A	C	B

Alan's the best in English.
Robert's the worst in Math.
Make sentences about: English/Math/
History/Spanish/Physics/Music.

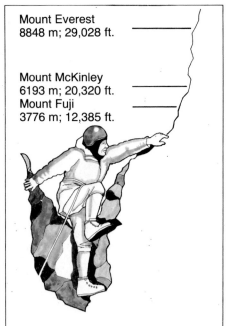

Toronto, Ontario
637 mm rainfall per year
25 in.

New Orleans, Louisiana
1340 mm; 56.7 in.

San Juan, Puerto Rico 1564 mm; 59.2 in.

They're all wet, ...

Mount Everest
8848 m; 29,028 ft.

Mount McKinley
6193 m; 20,320 ft.
Mount Fuji
3776 m; 12,385 ft.

They're all high, ...

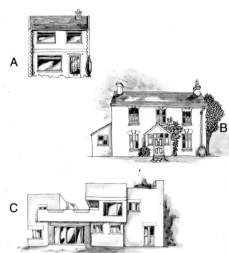

A

B

C

C's the most expensive.
A's the least expensive.
Make sentences using these words:
modern/beautiful/interesting.

71 Brutus Cray — the Greatest

Brutus Cray: I'm the greatest!

Reporter: You were the greatest, Brutus, but you're ten years older than Joe Freezer.

BC: Joe Freezer? I'm not afraid of Joe Freezer!

Rep.: Really?

BC: Listen! I've beaten him twice, and I'm going to beat him again.

Rep.: Are you sure?

BC: Sure? Of course, I'm sure.

Rep.: Some people say he's better than you.

BC: Listen! I've beaten all the best boxers, and Joe Freezer's one of the worst!

Rep.: Yes, but he's better than he was.

BC: Look, I'm stronger, faster, and more intelligent than he is. And I'm in better shape.

Rep.: Yes, but he knocked out Len Korton two months ago.

BC: Len Korton. That's nothing. I've KOed him three times!

Rep.: O.K., O.K., Brutus. Are you going to retire after this fight?

BC: Retire? No. I've been the champion for ten years, and I'm going to be the champ for another ten.

Rep.: Joe Freezer doesn't think so.

BC: Joe Freezer? Joe Freezer's the ugliest man in the world . . . after tonight he's going to need a new face.

Questions

Is Brutus older than Joe Freezer?
Is he afraid of Joe?
Has Brutus beaten him before?
Ask, "How many times?"

Has he beaten other boxers?
Ask, "Which boxers?"
Is Freezer worse than he was or better than he was?

Has Freezer beaten Len Korton?
Ask, "When?"
Is Brutus going to retire?
How long has he been the champion?

Exercise

A Joe Freezer/ ugly
B He/Brutus Cray
C He/the world

Write sentences like this:

A *Joe Freezer's very ugly.*
B *He's uglier than Brutus Cray.*
C *He's the ugliest man in the world.*

a Rockefeller/rich
b He/the President
c He/the world

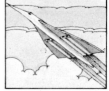

a Concorde/fast
b It/a Boeing
c It/the world

a Mount Everest/ high
b It/Mount McKinley
c It/the world

a Rolls-Royce/ comfortable
b It/Buick
c It/the world

a Brutus Cray/ good
b He/Joe Freezer
c He/the world

72 George and Brenda

George: Will you marry me, Brenda?
Brenda: Of course I will.
George: Is that a promise?
Brenda: Of course it is. I love you.

Brenda: Oh, George. I feel terribly tired.
George: Well, sit down. I'll do the dishes.
Brenda: Oh, thank you, darling . . . and, uh, I'm terribly thirsty.
George: All right. I'll bring you a Coke.

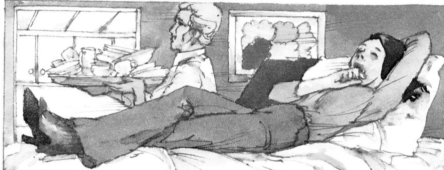

Brenda: George! Have you fixed that plug yet?
George: No, I haven't.
Brenda: Well, will you do it today?
George: Yes, I'll do it now. Where's the screwdriver?
Brenda: I really don't know.
George: Well, I can't find it.
Brenda: Don't worry, George. I'll do it tomorrow.

Brenda: Oh, George, we don't have anything for dinner.
George: That's all right. Let's eat out tonight.
Brenda: Oh, great. Where do you want to go?
George: Let's go to that new Italian restaurant down the street.

Brenda: George, dear.
George: Huh? What?
Brenda: You're drunk. I'll drive home.
George: No, I'm O.K. I'll drive.
Brenda: No, you won't. Give me the keys, George.

73 Everyday conversation

C: What's the matter? Why has the bus stopped?
D: There's been an accident.
C: There has? Again?
D: Yes, there have been three here this week.
C: I know. And it's only Wednesday.
D: It's the most dangerous corner I've ever seen.

this week
this month
this summer
this winter
this spring
this fall

corner
intersection
highway
hill
circle

E: Look at that girl!
F: What about her?
E: Look at her dress!
F: What about it?
E: It's the same as mine! That's what!
F: No, it isn't. It's different from yours.
E: Is it?
F: Yes. Hers is shorter than yours.

dress
skirt
coat
blazer

shorter
longer
newer
older
lighter
darker
cheaper
more expensive

G: Are you a new employee?
H: No, I'm not.
G: Oh. How long have you been here?
H: As long as you have.
G: Well, why haven't I seen you before?
H: I've been on vacation.

employee
student
editor
teacher

on vacation
away
sick
on a trip

I: Can I borrow $20? My check from my parents hasn't come yet.
J: I'm sorry, but I can't lend you anything. I'm broke.
I: What can I do?
J: Why don't you ask George? He's as rich as Rockefeller.

$20
$10
$5
50¢

George
Claudia
Tim
Bill
Connie

74 Something, nothing, anything, everything

A: I want some seats for Tuesday night. Are there any left?

B: No, there are no seats left. Every seat is reserved. I'm sorry.

C: Doctor, I think there's something in my eye. Everything looks funny.

D: Let me have a look . . . I can't see anything. No, I'm sure there's nothing there.

E: There's somebody in the other office!

F: I didn't hear anybody.

E: Take a look, please.

F: O.K. . . . No, there's nobody there. Everybody's gone home.

G: What are you looking for?

H: My pen. It's somewhere in this room.

G: Have you looked everywhere?

H: Yes, but I can't find it anywhere.

Exercise

something/someone/anything/anyone
There's *something* in my soup.
There's **. . .** in the other room.
Is there **. . .** in the refrigerator?
Is there **. . .** in the bathroom?
There isn't **. . .** in the cabinet.

anywhere/everywhere/nothing/something
I can't find it. I've looked **. . .** .
There's **. . .** to eat for dinner.
Would you like **. . .** to drink?
I want to stay home. I don't want to go **. . .** .

Study this

some	any?	no/not . . . any	every
something	anything?	nothing/not . . . anything	everything
somebody	anybody?	nobody/not . . . anybody	everybody
someone	anyone?	no one/not . . . anyone	everyone
somewhere	anywhere?	nowhere/not . . . anywhere	everywhere

75 Four lives

Herbert Burke, James Brody, Gina Rossi, and Charles Phillips all went to the same school. They finished elementary school in 1959 and high school in 1965. They've had very different careers.

Herbie Burke became a politician six years ago. He's very successful. He bought a country house five years ago and bought a Jaguar at the same time. He's been a Senator for six years. He's had his house and car for five years.

Jimmy Brody is a criminal. He robbed a bank in 1980 and escaped to a Pacific island. He bought a luxury yacht the next year. He's still on the island. He's been there since 1980. He's had his yacht since 1981.

Gina Rossi and Charlie Phillips fell in love at school. He gave her a ring when they finished high school. She wears it every day, and she's never taken it off. They got married in 1972, and they're still in love. They moved to Arizona in 1979.

Questions

When did Herbie Burke become a politician?
When did he buy a country house?
When did he buy a Jaguar?
How long has he been a Senator?
How long has he had his house?
How long has he had his car?

Questions

When did Jimmy rob a bank?
Where did he escape to?
What did he buy?
When did he buy it?
Where is he now?
How long has he been there?
How long has he had his yacht?

Questions

When did Gina and Charlie fall in love?
When did he give her the ring?
Has she ever taken it off?
When did they get married?
Are they still in love?
When did they move to Arizona?
How long has she had the ring?
How long have they been married?
How long have they been in Arizona?

Exercise

He's been there *since* 1975.
They've been there *for* five years.
Complete these sentences:
1 She's had that watch . . . three weeks.

2 We've been here . . . January.
3 I've had my camera . . . two years.
4 They've been married . . . 1974.
5 He's had his car . . . two months.
6 Jorge's been in the United States . . . March.

77 Saturday night at the Electric Disco

It's Saturday night at the Electric Disco in Brooklyn. It's time for the Electric Disco Dance Contest. The new hit song, "I Have Survived," is playing very loud. All of the couples are dancing. Some of them are great dancers! The judges are watching the couples. One of the judges is the famous movie star, John Revolta.

All of the judges are pleased. They have chosen two couples for the last dance. Both of the couples are dancing beautifully, and the judges are looking carefully. In a moment they're going to announce the winners.

The judges have voted, and John Revolta has announced the result. The winners are Tina Rivera and Joe Costas. Neither of them are from Brooklyn. Both of them are from Manhattan. Neither of them have been in a contest before. All of the other dancers are cheering or booing. Some of them are happy with the winners, but the others aren't. But none of them are bored. It has been another fantastic Saturday night at the Electric Disco!

Exercise

One of them is a policeman.

Both of them are policemen.

Neither of them are policemen.

Some of them are happy.

All of them are happy.

None of them are happy.

. . . nurse.

. . . nurses.

. . . nurses.

. . . fat.

. . . fat.

. . . fat.

The Weekly Gazette

20¢

Wednesday, May 20, 1983

Marion, North Carolina

SENSATIONAL JEWEL ROBBERY

$25,000 STOLEN

There was a twenty-five thousand dollar jewel robbery on Elm Street last Tuesday. The thieves threw a rock through the window of Williston & Company and stole necklaces, rings, and watches worth $25,000. Mr. William Williston, the owner of the shop, was working in his office when it happened. The police are looking for three suspects. The thieves drove away in a stolen Toyota Celica. The police have not found the getaway car yet.

Mr. Williston will give a reward of $1000 to anyone with information about the thieves. Get in touch with the local police station.

Everest Expedition Fails

An international team of climbers in the Himalayas wanted to reach the top of Mount Everest yesterday, but they failed because the weather was too bad. They had to postpone the climb until next week. The weather has been the worst since 1979. The three climbers are from Mexico, Japan, and the United States.

Hollywood Divorce Case

Taylor leaves Bertram

Richard Taylor, the British actor, is going to divorce his wife, Liza Bertram. They have been married for thirteen years and have lived in Hollywood since 1970. (They also have houses in Switzerland, Brazil, and England.) Several people have seen Taylor with fashion model Sally Hunter recently. He has been married four times. He refused to speak to our reporter yesterday.

RUNAWAY TEENAGER

Janis Roberts, 15 years old, of 1647 Sunrise Road, Marion, left her home last week. She was on her way to school, and nobody has seen her since. Janis's friend, Polly Reyes, talked to the police yesterday.

Janis was wearing blue jeans, a green T-shirt, a white raincoat, and tan boots. She has short blond hair and blue eyes. Please call 461-4600 with any information.

79 Everyday conversation

K: Can I help you?
L: Yes, I want to send some flowers to my mother in Chicago.
K: What kind of flowers would you like?
L: Well, what do you recommend?
K: Roses are very nice at this time of year.
L: O.K. A dozen red roses, please.
K: Would you like to include a message?
L: Yes. Just say, "Happy Birthday, Mom. Love, Cindy."

roses
tulips
carnations
daisies

a dozen (12)
half a dozen (6)
two dozen (24)
ten (10)

M: Mrs. Conner?
N: Yes, Paul?
M: This is a present for you.
N: A present for me? What a nice surprise. Can I open it now?
M: Yes, of course.
N: Ooh! Candy! I love candy. Thank you very, very much, Paul.
M: Thank *you*, Mrs. Conner. You've been very kind to me.

a present
a gift
something

candy
cookies
perfume
fruit

O: I'd like to say goodbye to everybody.
P: When are you leaving?
O: Tomorrow morning.
P: Let's get together tonight.
O: I'm afraid I can't.
P: Oh, come on.
O: No, really. I've got *so* much to do.

tomorrow morning
tomorrow afternoon
the day after
 tomorrow
next week
in two days
in a few hours

Q: It's been a wonderful party. Thanks very much.
R: But you can't go yet! The party's just beginning!
Q: I'm sorry, but I really have to.
R: Why?
Q: Because I have to catch the last train.
R: Don't be silly. I'll give you a ride. Where are you going?
Q: Montreal!
R: Oh. Well, thanks for coming.

Montreal
Caracas
Tokyo
Istanbul
Rio

Pensión San José
Hamburgo 243
Zona Rosa
Mexico 5, D.F.
August 23

Darling John,

I've missed you very much. I've been so lonely this week because I haven't seen you for a long time – a whole month! I've learned a lot of Spanish. I've worked hard and I haven't been out too much. Last night I had to do a lot of homework, and I'm tired today.

Mexico City is much larger than Cleveland, and it's more interesting. I think it's the best city I've ever been to. There's too much traffic and smog, and there aren't enough restaurants with American food, but I like it. All of my teachers are very nice. Some of them are better than others. None of them speak English to us, so we all have to speak Spanish.

Anyway, I have to study now. I'll write again soon. I promise.

All my love,

Mary xxx

P.S. You haven't written to me in two weeks. Please write.

Dear Joe,
      Mom,
      Dad,
      Anne,

I've missed | you | very much. | I've been | lonely | this week because I haven't seen
| *home* | *a lot.* | | *sad* |
| *the family* | *so much.* | | *miserable* |

you for | a month. | And I haven't heard from you since | January. | I've learned | a lot of
| *a long time.* | | *Christmas.* | | *a little*
| *a year.* | | *Easter.* |

English | this week. I've | worked | hard, | and I haven't been out | much. | Last night I
French | | *studied* | *a lot,* | | *many times.*
Spanish | | | *only a little,* | | *at all.*
| | | | | *too much.*

had to | study a lot, | and I'm | tired | today. New York is | more | expensive than | Tokyo,
| *write a composition,* | | *sleepy* | | *less* | | *Rio,*
| *learn a dialog,* | | | | | | *Lima,*

but it's | more | interesting. | I think it's the | best | city I've ever | been to. | There | 's | too
| *less* | *exciting.* | | *worst* | | *seen.* | | *are*
| | *beautiful.* | | | | *visited.*

much | traffic | and there aren't enough | restaurants | with | Latin American music, | but | I
many | *dogs* | | *bars* | | *Japanese beer,* | *and*
| *pollution* | | *discos* | | *Brazilian music,*
| *people*

like | it. | All | of my teachers are | good | and none of them speak | Japanese | to me, so I
love | | *Some* | | *fantastic* | | *Spanish*
hate | | *None* | | *excellent* | | *Portuguese*
| | | | *terrible* | | *Arabic*

have to speak English. | Well, | I | really have to | go to bed now. I'll write again
| *Anyway,* | | *want to*
| | | *need to*

tomorrow . . . | I promise.
soon . . .
on Wednesday . . .
next week . . .

All my love,
Yours,
With love,
Love,

Vocabulary

This vocabulary contains all the words in the student's book, and the number of the unit where they first occur.

A

a 1A
about 15
Acapulco 31
accident 38
accountant 8
astronaut 8
ache 39
across 25
action 12
actor 12
actress 12
address 19
advanced 20
advice 46
advisor 20
afraid 47
after 26
afternoon 15
again 45
agent 6
ago 51
air 64
airline 53
airport 28
album 57
all 28
all right 15
alone 32
along 25
a lot 7
already 65
always 35
am 1A
ambulance 55
American 2A
an 3A
and 1B
angry 5B
animal 29
announce 77
another 30
answer 32
any 6
anybody 46
anything 10
anyway 23
anywhere 74
apartment 6
appetizer 11
apple 3A
appointment 44
April 41
Arabic 14
architect 33
are 1B
area 52
Arizona 75
arm 67
army 52
around 60

arrive 40
artist 34
as 20
ashtray 3B
ask 22
asleep 47
astronaut 8
at 7
Athens 59
athletic 14
Atlantic City 51
attack (v) 56
August 41
Australia 65
automatic 13
average 68
aviation 53
away 47

B

back (part of body) 39
back 45
backache 39
backyard 13
bad 20
badly 38
bag 18
baked 11
bakery 45
balcony 6
ballet 34
banana 10
bank 7
bar 13
barber 41
barman 47
baseball 14
bath 32
bathrobe 43
bathroom 6
be (v) 12
beach 20
bean 11
beard 60
beat (v) 71
beautiful 5A
beauty 50
beauty salon 39
because 25
become 53
bed 3B
bedroom 6
beef 11
beer 7
before 67
begin 52
beginning 20
behind 25
bellman 4B

belt 24
bend 25
Bermuda 42
best 20
best wishes 20
better 68
between 25
beverage 11
bicycle 9
big 5B
bike 57
bill 31
billionaire 53
biography 53
birthdate 29
birthday 44
black 8
blazer 73
blond 78
blouse 8
blue 8
Blue Ridge
    Mountains 52
boat 48
bone 55
boo (v) 77
book 6
boot 15
booth 7
bored 63
boring 20
borrow 23
boss 9
Boston 15
both 28
bottle 6
bourbon 7
boutique 39
bowl 10
box 10
boxer 71
boy 25
boyfriend 60
brake 55
brandy 19
Brazil 1B
Brazilian 80
bread 7
break (v) 52
breakfast 32
bride 28
bridge 66
bring 19
British 78
broiled 11
broke 16
Brooklyn 41
brother 9
brown 8
brush (v) 35
bucket 63
build (v) 53
building 6
bullet 47
burn (v) 52
bus 3A

bus stop 7
(on) business
    2A
busy 20
but 14
butcher 45
butter 7
button 18
buy (v) 25
by 60
bye 19

C

cabinet 6
cafeteria 33
cake 11
California 8
Californian 60
call 39
calmly 47
Cambridge 60
camera 12
campaign 53
campus 60
can 14
Canada 1B
candy 15
canteen 33
capital 52
captain 8
car 3A
Caracas 79
career 75
careful 38
carefully 38
careless 38
carelessly 38
carnation 28
carrot 11
carry 19
carton 17
case (legal) 78
cashier 4B
casino 33
cassette 13
cassette player
    13
cassette recorder
    19
cat 55
catch (v) 49
catsup 7
cauliflower 11
caviar 33
center 59
centigrade/C 68
central 41
cereal 33
ceremony 34
certainly 11
chain 24
chair 3A
champagne 27
champion 71
(a) change 54

change 31
change (v) 31
channel 26
charge 59
cheap 5A
check 19
checkbook 63
check into 58
cheer (v) 77
cheese 10
Chicago 27
chicken 11
children 8
China 41
Chinese 2B
chocolate 11
chops 11
chose 77
Christmas 35
church 27
cigar 9
cigarette 17
cigarette lighter
    13
circle 73
city 59
class 20
classical 18
classroom 60
clean (v) 63
clearly 61
Cleveland 20
climb 52
climber 52
clock 3B
close (v) 12
close up 26
clothes 30
club 33
coal 69
coat 18
cocktail 28
code 59
coffee 2A
coffee shop 7
coin 31
cola 11
cold 5A
(a) cold 39
collect 59
college 67
Colombia 41
color 8
come 8
comedy 26
comfortable 13
company 36
comparison 68
competent 39
composition 20
computer 29
computer
    dating 29
concert 15
conductor 51
cone 3A

Connecticut 60
contact 58
contest 77
contestant 34
continuous 59
control 61
convenient 31
conversation 7
cook 4B
cook (v) 14
cookie 15
corner 55
cotton 24
cough 51
could (request) 7
could (ability) 57
country 48
couple 77
courses 55
cousin 67
cowboy 47
cracker 49
crash (v) 49
crazy 27
cream 2A
criminal 75
crowd 64
cry (v) 62
cup 3A
customer 11
Customs 17
Customs officer 1
cut 2B

D

dad 80
daddy 14
daily 78
daisy 79
Dallas 52
dance 23
dance (v) 21
dancing 71
dangerous 58
dark 24
darling 72
date 44
daughter 9
day 32
Dear... 20
deaf 63
December 29
declare 17
deep 68
degree 68
delicious 20
denim 24
dentist 34
department 51
deposit 59
design 53
desk 46
Des Moines 59
dessert 11
destroy 52

iron (v) 14
is 1A
island 75
Istanbul 79
it (pronoun) 3A
it (obj) 12
Italian 2B
itinerary 65

J

jacket 8
January 41
Japan 1B
Japanese 2B
jar 10
jazz 29
jeans 8
jewel 78
jeweller 78
jewelry 78
job 4B
jockey 37
join (v) 69
journey 44
judge 77
juice 11
July 41
June 41
just 31

K

Kansas 55
key 3A
kicker 52
kid (v) 27
kill (v) 47
kilometer/km 68
kind 31
kiss (v) 12
kitchen 6
knife 3A
knit 29
knock out
    (v)/K.O. 71
know 22
Korean 20

L

ladder 61
lady 24
lake 26
lamb 11
land (v) 61
language 14
language school
    37
large 6
last 7
Las Vegas 31
late 25
later 15
Latin American
    80

laugh (v) 12
laundromat 7
laundry 41
lazy 38
learn 40
learner 38
least 70
leather 24
leave (v) 27
left 7
leg 52
legend 47
lemon 3A
less 68
lesson 44
let 17
let me see 43
letter 22
library 60
lie 25
life 13
lifeboat 49
light (adj) 5B
light (n) 12
light (color) 24
lighter 13
like (v) 29
likes (n) 29
like (What's it
    like?) 42
limousine 15
line 25
liquor 17
listen 29
little 27
living room 6
lobster 27
local 26
lock 56
London 2B
lonely 22
long 5A
long (time) 73
long distance 59
look (v) 8
look at 8
look for 23
look into 12
Los Angeles 2A
lose (v) 28
lost 49
lot 10
loud 77
Louisiana 68
love (v) 15
lovely 18
luck 58
lucky 27
luggage 19
lunch 32
luxury 75

M

magazine 6
magician 60

mail 29
main course 11
make (n) 19
make (v) 28
male 56
man 13
manager 4B
Manhattan 77
manufacture (v)
    53
many 66
Maracaibo 59
March 40
marital 29
market 36
market research
    36
marry 30
Massachusetts
    60
master 34
master of
    ceremonies
    (MC) 34
match 49
math 68
matter 39
may 4A
May 29
Mayan 60
mayor 52
me 2A
meal 54
mean (v) 44
meat 10
mechanic 4B
medicine 52
medium 11
meet (v) 15
melon 11
mend (v) 72
menu 11
message 59
meter/m 68
Mexican 2B
Mexico 1B
Mexico City 20
Miami 20
microphone 12
middle-aged 55
midnight 33
mile 53
milk 7
millimeter/mm
    68
million 53
millionaire 9
mine (pronoun)
    18
miner 69
minus 68
minute 19
mirror 63
miserable 80
miss (v) 47
mission 58

mixed 11
model 78
modern 70
mom 66
moment 37
mommy 14
Monday 23
money 16
month 42
Montreal 79
moon 44
mop 63
more 14
morning 15
Moscow 58
most 70
mother 9
mother-in-law
    27
motorcycle 16
mountain 52
Mount Everest
    68
Mount
    McKinley 68
move (v) 12
movie 15
Mr. 4A
Mrs. 4A
Ms. 5B
much 7
mushroom 10
music 29
mustache 25
mustard 7
my 4A

N

name 4A
nationality 58
near 7
nearly 45
necklace 24
need (v) 30
neither 77
never 35
new 5A
New Haven 60
New Jersey 41
New Orleans 31
news 26
newspaper 23
New York 2B
next 27
nice 6
nickel 31
night 18
nightclub 21
nightgown 43
nine 36
nine-thirty 32
ninth 34
no 1A
no (not any) 74

nobody 46
noise 64
noisily 38
noisy 38
none 77
noon 40
normal 44
normally 54
North Carolina
    78
not 1A
nothing 33
November 41
now 12
nowadays 35
nowhere 74
number 4A
nurse 52
nylon 23

O

obey (v) 69
occasionally 35
occupation 29
ocean 42
o'clock 15
October 41
of 11
of course 9
off 12
office 19
officer 17
often 35
oh 1A
Ohio 20
oil 10
oil-drilling
    company 53
O.K. 7
old 5A
omelette 11
on 2A
once 36
one 6
onion 10
only 13
open (v) 12
opera 36
operator 59
opposite 55
or 35
orange (color) 8
orange (fruit) 3A
orchestra 42
ordinary 32
Oregon 41
other 23
our 4A
ours 18
out 12
out of 25
outside 25
over there 4A
owner 78

P

Pacific Ocean 49
package 51
pair 15
palace 60
Palm Beach 30
pan 6
pants 24
pardon 2A
parent 28
Paris 2B
park (n) 20
parking lot 56
party 23
pass (v) 7
passenger 53
passion 54
passport 16
patient 52
pay 43
pea 10
peach 43
pen 3A
pencil 63
Pennsylvania 69
penny 31
pension 69
people 25
pepper 7
per 53
perfume 17
personal 29
Philadelphia 31
Phoenix 20
phone 7
photo 57
photocopy 46
photograph 48
physics 55
piano 57
picnic 23
picture 20
pie 11
piece 15
pigeon 60
pilot 4B
pink 8
pistachio 43
pitcher 10
pizza 10
place 27
plane 15
plate 3A
play (v) 14
please 2A
pleased 77
plug (n) 72
plus 68
pocket 63
police 52
policeman 4B
politician 75
pollution 64
polyester 24
poor 5A

Irregular verbs

Infinitive form	Past tense	Past participle	Infinitive form	Past tense	Past participle	Infinitive form	Past tense	Past participle
be	was/were	been	get	got	got	see	saw	seen
beat	beat	beaten	give	gave	given	sell	sold	sold
become	became	become	go	went	gone	send	sent	sent
begin	began	begun	grow	grew	grown	shine	shone	shone
bite	bit	bitten	have	had	had	shoot	shot	shot
break	broke	broken	hear	heard	heard	show	showed	shown
bring	brought	brought	hide	hid	hidden	shut	shut	shut
build	built	built	hit	hit	hit	sing	sang	sung
buy	bought	bought	hurt	hurt	hurt	sit	sat	sat
catch	caught	caught	keep	kept	kept	sleep	slept	slept
choose	chose	chosen	know	knew	known	speak	spoke	spoken
come	came	come	leave	left	left	spend	spent	spent
cost	cost	cost	lend	lent	lent	stand	stood	stood
cut	cut	cut	let	let	let	steal	stole	stolen
do	did	done	light	lit	lit	swim	swam	swum
drink	drank	drunk	lose	lost	lost	take	took	taken
drive	drove	driven	make	made	made	teach	taught	taught
eat	ate	eaten	mean	meant	meant	tear	tore	torn
fall	fell	fallen	meet	met	met	tell	told	told
feel	felt	felt	pay	paid	paid	think	thought	thought
fight	fought	fought	put	put	put	throw	threw	thrown
find	found	found	read	read	read	wake	woke	woken
fly	flew	flown	ride	rode	ridden	wear	wore	worn
forbid	forbade	forbidden	ring	rang	rung	win	won	won
forget	forgot	forgotten	run	ran	run	write	wrote	written
freeze	froze	frozen	say	said	said			